BADASS
AFFIRMATIONS

Published by Mango Publishing Group, a division of Mango Media Inc.

Cover, Layout & Design: Morgane Leoni

For permission requests, please contact the publisher at:

Mango Publishing Group
2850 Douglas Road, 3rd Floor
Coral Gables, FL 33134 U.S.A.
info@mango.bz

For special orders, quantity sales, course adoptions and corporate sales, please email the publisher at sales@mango.bz. For trade and wholesale sales, please contact Ingram Publisher Services at:
customer.service@ingramcontent.com or +1.800.509.4887.

Badass Affirmations: The Wit and Wisdom of Wild Women

Library of Congress Cataloging-in-Publication.
ISBN: (p) 978-1-63353-752-1, (e) 978-1-63353-753-8
Library of Congress Control Number: 2018937912
BISAC: SEL004000 – SELF-HELP / Affirmations

Printed in the United States of America

BADASS
AFFIRMATIONS

The Wit and Wisdom of Wild Women

Becca Anderson

Mango Publishing

CORAL GABLES, FL

Also by Becca Anderson

Badass Women Give the Best Advice: Everything You Need to Know About Love and Life

Real Life Mindfulness: Meditations for a Calm and Quiet Mind

Think Happy to Stay Happy: The Awesome Power of Learned Optimism

Prayers for Hard Times: Reflections, Meditations and Inspirations of Hope and Comfort

The Book of Awesome Women: Boundary Breakers, Freedom Fighters, Sheroes and Female Firsts

Every Day Thankful: 365 Blessings, Graces and Gratitudes

This book is dedicated to my sister,
who never ceases to inspire me.

This book is dedicated to my mother,
who taught me how to bounce back from a setback.

And this book is dedicated to you, dear reader,
for your possibilities are endless,
and you can do anything you set your mind to.

Contents

Introduction

All About Affirmations

If you're anything like me, there are always aspects of your life or your personality that you're working to improve. After all, nobody's perfect—that's part of the beauty of life. We all make mistakes, we all have bad habits, we all make bad choices sometimes, and that's okay. In fact, that's great! But if you do want to continue learning and improving, it's probably not a great idea to just keep doing the same thing you've been doing for years. It's time to try something new.

This is where affirmations come in. Affirmations are positive statements that you make out loud, every day, to help you shift your mindset in a positive and productive way. These statements can be about literally anything. For example, if you are trying to increase your self-confidence, you could say something like, "My self-confidence increases every day." Or if, let's say, you just had a bad breakup and you're trying to shift your focus from your dating life (or lack thereof) to your career—then you could say to yourself, "I will focus on improving my job prospects," or, "I am completely focused on my work." It's all about what changes you want to make—how you want to improve your mindset and, ultimately, your life.

Now, one of the main benefits of affirmations is that they help you to change how you think—over time. You won't wake up one morning, say to yourself that you're going to be happy from now on, and then have the best day of your life every day until you die. (Well, you probably won't, anyway—I suppose anything is possible.) But if you commit to taking five minutes of your morning to stand in front of the mirror, look yourself in the eye, and tell yourself that you are a beautiful, capable person who will achieve all she is working for, you'll find that after a couple of weeks, you're actually starting to believe yourself. Maybe you'll stop cringing every time you look in the mirror, or maybe you'll start to notice all of the small steps you're making toward your big goals—the steps that have been made easier now that you know, and I mean *really* know, that you're capable of anything you set your mind to.

Affirmations aren't magic spells. You can't just say that you're going to advance in your career and sit in your chair staring at a blank computer screen every day—you have to work your ass off and take advantage of the chance opportunities that come around. You can't just tell yourself that you're going to love your family members better and then proceed to ignore them every time they come near—you have to actually listen when they talk and respond patiently and kindly. What I'm saying is, if you don't follow up on your affirmations with actions, not much in your life will really change. I mean, it makes sense. Empty words are useless. But affirmations *are* the first step to a better morning, to an improved mindset—to a you that you actually like to be around.

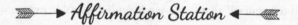

Affirmation Station

Every chapter of this book is full of mini-sections I like to call ***Affirmation Stations***. Each station has a few examples of affirmations that you can use to start your journey toward self-improvement.

Now, not every affirmation is for every person. If your goal is to be happy single, for example, you shouldn't say, "I will love my partner well"; rather, you should say, "I am happy and excited to be independent." If you want to change your career or find a new job, you shouldn't say, "I am happy at my job,"—you should say, "I am capable of making positive changes." My recommendation is to pull out your old highlighters or some colorful pens and mark the affirmations that you want to use. Find sticky notes in your favorite color and post some of them on your bathroom mirror, on the bottom edge of your computer screen, or on your fridge. Only use the ones that reflect your own goals. And keep this book in a place you pass by every day, so that you can pull out new affirmations when your goals evolve and change—just as you do.

There Is No "Try"

You may notice that most of the affirmations in this book start with something along the lines of "I am" or "I will," not "I want to" or "I'll try to." That's because in order to shift your mindset, you need to use strong words. If you say "I'll *try* to be more positive," you're making it easier to avoid hard changes. If you say "I *want* to inspire others," you're repeating empty words. These statements don't encourage you; they trap you in your old self. Because aren't you already trying to be more positive? Yes, that's why you picked up this book. Don't you already know that you want to inspire others? Of course you do. There's no thought-shifting there—no improvement.

When you say "I *will* be more positive," though, you're locking yourself into making that improvement. You've made a commitment to yourself, one that you aren't going to take likely.

When you say "I *am* inspiring others," you remind yourself of the truth. You start to see your actions in a new way; you know they affect others positively. And you start to see yourself in a new light—you know the inspiration you are, the inspiration you were always meant to be.

It doesn't matter if your chosen affirmations aren't quite accurate yet. What matters is that they reflect your end goal—where you want to be, not where you see yourself now. They're instruments of change, and they have to be a little sharper and more forceful than your natural language. So, as you continue your odyssey toward a positive mindset, an improved life, give yourself a leg up and say "I will." Oh—and say it out loud. No one else has to be around when you do it, anyway, and even a whisper is a more powerful weapon against internal negativity and stagnancy than timid silence. You have nothing to lose and everything to gain.

▼▼▼▼▼▼▼▼▼▼▼▼▼▼▼▼▼▼▼▼▼▼▼▼▼▼▼▼▼▼▼▼

The Art of Self-Affirmation:
How to Use This Book

Pick up the book, randomly open to a quote, and let those words be your guiding thought for the day. If you are REALLY resonating to this power-thought, keep using it every day and let it become your mantra.

Use these inspired ideas in speeches, on your bulletin board, in your email signature, as your Twitter handle, or on your social media. Hey, if it is your favorite ever Big Thought, get a tattoo on your inner wrist where you see it all the time and are reminded of your personal worth and of the great big, beautiful world we all live in.

Read a few and really "power up" for your day—sort of like getting a booster shot in word form. If you are getting ready to do a presentation, a sales pitch, an interview for your dream job, your next YouTube taping, or any very important date, this affirmation can be the wind in your sails.

Always remember this, you have to think happy to be happy! Xoxox

▲▲▲▲▲▲▲▲▲▲▲▲▲▲▲▲▲▲▲▲▲▲▲▲▲▲▲▲▲▲▲▲

So What Are These Quotes For?

Just about a third of this book is made of words that I didn't come up, with from women who are far more successful, well-known, and inspiring than I am. That's not self-deprecation—I have my fair share of accomplishments—it's just a fact. They've done a lot, and they've become a lot. I wanted to include them for a couple of reasons.

First, the more women whose words you and I can relate to, the less alone we'll feel. This book is here to encourage and uplift you, and what better way to do that than to show you just how many women you can understand and connect with—women that you haven't even met! These women represent people from all over the world, fighting for causes from a wide spectrum, racking up a myriad of unprecedented achievements. And they're just like you: human beings who cried when they were born and worked hard every day since that first tear to get where they ended up. It really is a small world, after all.

I also wanted to show you that there's no one right way to live your life. The women quoted in this book are all wildly different, one-of-a-kind individuals. You won't agree with all of them—hey,

I don't even agree with all of them, and I wrote the book—but that's great! They're all still notable, successful, and impressive individuals, each with something of her own to share. We can be encouraged by their successes while we strive for our own. They weren't perfect, just as we aren't perfect … but they didn't let that stop them. In fact, they owned their imperfections—after all, their imperfections helped to make them who they were, who they became. And these incredible women made all of their accomplishments, won all of their awards, broke all of their boundaries, in a lot of different ways—and we can too.

Finally, these women are trendsetters. They're wave-makers, tradition-breakers, and world-shakers. And they all started at the bottom. They took what they had—and in some cases, that really wasn't much!—and they used it to grow themselves into inspirations, whether that was what they'd always meant to do, or they got there completely by accident. And you know what? That's exactly what you can do, too.

So grab those highlighters, a few colorful pens, and any semblance of a can-do attitude that you can scrounge up, and start flipping pages. I know you've got this. You're ready to affirm yourself to victory.

Journaling to Get You Started

At the end of this book are twenty thought exercises in the form of journal prompts. These prompts are intended to help you think through your goals and aspirations—and then think through practical and reasonable ways to meet those goals.

Here are a few examples of the journal prompts you will find in the back of this book:

- Pick an inspiring quote. Why does it inspire you? How will you take advantage of that inspiration today?

- How can you realistically lead a healthier life? What small steps will you take each day to implement these ideas?

- What changes do you want to see in your love life? Which affirmations will help you make those changes?

As you can see, these prompts will help you take the content of this book—the quotes, the badass bios, the affirmations—and put them to some real use. They're a springboard, a way to get you started. Once you've gone through these prompts, I suggest that you continue journaling your goals, your progress, and your affirmations and quotes. Be realistic in what you can achieve. Don't overestimate your abilities—but don't underestimate your drive, either. You can be the change you want to see in the world, and you can make the changes that you want to have in your life.

Chapter One

What's Wrong with Being Confident?

In a day and age when women are still fighting for equal pay for equal (and sometimes—dare I say—better) work, it's easy to see how we might have trouble with our self-esteem. After all, we're still shaking off the side effects of hundreds of years of training to be seen but not heard, to serve but not be served. But thanks to modern feminism, women are again fighting back against the archaic, "traditional" idea that a woman's role is to simply be an in-home cook, personal maid, and smiling living-room ornament—today, we women tackle work and play, motherhood and muscle, beauty and bossiness. After all, what better quality than bossiness is there for the accomplished bosses and leaders of the world?

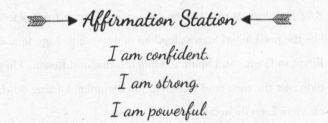

And confidence is not a new feminine trait. In fact, it's been around for just as long as suppression has. Look at anyone from the biblical Esther to France's Joan of Arc and ask yourself whether they didn't walk with their shoulders back and their heads held high, even with the limited power afforded to them by their patriarchal societies. And they aren't the only ones to take hold of power despite being looked down upon just for their gender. After all, the longest-reigning British monarch, Queen Elizabeth II, happens to be both female and still on top, and the United Kingdom isn't the only sovereign state to have had a woman in charge. Ellen Johnson Sirleaf, who was elected President of Liberia in 2006, was Africa's first elected chief executive—and when her term ended in 2018, she left her post peacefully and gave Liberia its first peaceful transition of power since 1944. And Ellen Johnson Sirleaf isn't the only symbol for African women taking up the reins of democracy—women in Rwanda, although they still face terrible challenges, make up well over half of the Rwandan legislature. Women have ruled all over, from places like the pre-United States kingdom of Hawaii to Nigeria and Egypt to France and Spain to China, India, and Russia. They didn't let the men (and even the other women) looking down on them keep them down.

Affirmation Station

I am capable.

I am a leader.

I go after what I want.

It doesn't take a monarch to have confidence, though. Anyone can know their own worth, as the wide range of women quoted below will show you. These women know who they are, they accept who they are, and they love who they are—and you can too. No one has to tell you that just surviving in this world full of violence and negativity is an accomplishment, but you do have to tell yourself. You need to affirm your dignity every day, to remind yourself that you are capable of anything and everything you set your mind to. Because, let's face it—you are.

Affirmation Station

I am successful.

I am worthy.

I respect myself.

You are just like the women quoted below. You will not bow. You will not be changed against your will. You will not be moved. Because deep down, we both know that who you are is exactly who you're supposed to be.

I thank God I am endowed with such qualities that if I were turned out of the Realm in my petticoat I were able to live in any place in Christendom.

—**Elizabeth I**, Queen of England for forty-four years, who casually steered England through one of its most peaceful and prosperous times, all while charming her people and cleverly evading claims of feminine inadequacy; she vowed to never lose her head in love after seeing and learning about the painful love life of her mother and, especially, her father

I'm so popular it's scary sometimes. I suppose I'm just everybody's type.

—**Catherine Deneuve**, an Academy Award-nominated French actress whose international career has stretched for over half a century

In spite of honest efforts to annihilate my I-ity, or merge it in what the world doubtless considers my better half, I still find myself a self-subsisting and alas! self-seeking me.

—**Jane Welsh Carlyle**, eighteenth-century author known for her wit and sass; she wrote her first novel (and a five-act tragedy!) while still in her teenage years

Some people say I'm attractive. I say I agree.

—**Cybill Shepherd**, actress and the winner of three Golden Globe awards; she began singing at the age of five and hasn't let anyone or anything stop her since

I am growing handsome very fast indeed! I expect I shall be the belle of Amherst when I reach my 17th year. I don't doubt that I shall have perfect crowds of admirers at that age. Then how I shall delight to make them await my bidding, and with what delight shall I witness their suspense while I make my final decision.

—**Emily Dickinson**, voluntary recluse and writer of nearly eighteen hundred poems; though she never cared much whether they were published, her family and close friends did (to our great benefit!)

≫⟶ *Affirmation Station* ⟵≪

I am beautiful.

I am attractive.

I love myself.

I came out of the womb a diva. All it means is you know your worth as a woman.

—**Cyndi Lauper**, singer, songwriter, and actress who has won two Academy Awards and been honored with fifteen Academy Award nominations; her songwriting for Broadway's 2013 hit musical *Kinky Boots* (which won a total of six Tonys) made her the first solo woman to receive the Tony Award for Best Original Score

The world is wide, and I would not waste my life in friction when it could be turned into momentum.

—**Frances Willard**, an educator and temperance activist who helped found the national Prohibition Party and served as president of the Woman's Christian Temperance Union; she campaigned for women's suffrage across the country and traveled the world fighting the international drug trade

My master had power and law on his side; I had a determined will. There is might in each.

—**Harriet Ann Jacobs**, who spent seven years hiding alone in a three-foot-tall nook in her grandmother's house in order to save her children and herself from the wrongs of those who owned her; after she escaped and returned to her children, who had finally been sent north, she became a nurse and a writer, telling her moving story so that all could learn about the horrors of slavery

I will not be vanquished.

—**Rose Kennedy**, matriarch of a family made up partially of politicians; she was their anchor and assisted in many of their political (and personal!) victories

I used to be Snow White, but I drifted.

—**Mae West**, actress, playwright, and burlesque performer; she was arrested for her then-scandalous Broadway show *Sex*, which she wrote, directed, and produced herself

➤➤➤ ➤ *Affirmation Station* ◄ ◄◄◄

I will succeed.

I believe in myself.

I achieve whatever I put my mind to.

Vinegar he poured on me all his life; I am well marinated; how can I be honey now?

—**Tillie Olsen**, a groundbreaking fiction author and high school dropout (later awarded nine honorary doctorates!) who often wrote about the lives of women, minorities, and the working poor; she inspired many collegiate-level Women's Studies programs throughout the United States and beyond

Prudent people are very happy; 'tis an exceeding fine thing, that's certain, but I was born without it, and shall retain to my day of death the humour of saying what I think.

—**Lady Mary Wortley Montagu**, letter writer, essayist, and world-traveling poet; her face had been ravaged by smallpox as a child, so when she witnessed smallpox inoculation in Turkey, she jumped at the chance to inoculate her children against smallpox and brought the practice back to her native England

It is indeed, a trial to maintain the virtue of humility when one can't help being right.

—**Judith Martin** (a.k.a. "Miss Manners"), author of *Miss Manners' Guide to Excruciatingly Correct Behavior*

I just throw dignity against the wall and think only of the game.

—**Suzanne Lenglen**, the world's first professional female tennis player; she popularized women's tennis as a spectator sport

▼▼▼▼▼▼▼▼▼▼▼▼▼▼▼▼▼▼▼▼▼▼▼▼▼▼▼▼▼▼▼

Badass to the Bone:

Suzanne Lenglen

Suzanne was born in Paris in 1899. As a child, she was frail and suffered from many health problems, including chronic asthma. Tennis, her father decided, would build up her strength and benefit her health. She first tried her hand at the game in 1910, on the family tennis court, and her father began to train her to play competitively. Only four years later, at age fourteen, Lenglen made it to the final of the 1914 French Championships (now the French Open); she lost to reigning champion Marguerite

Broquedis, but later that spring won the World Hard Court Championships at Saint-Cloud, Paris, on her fifteenth birthday, making her the youngest person in tennis history to this day to win a major championship.

Lenglen made her Wimbledon debut in 1919, taking on seven-time champion Dorothea Douglass Chambers in the final. The historic match was played before eight thousand onlookers, including King George V and his Queen-Consort, Mary of Teck. Lenglen won the match; however, the young woman's skill wasn't the only subject to draw notice and public comment. The media squawked about her dress, which revealed her forearms and ended above the calf; at the time, others competed in body-covering ensembles. The staid British were also shocked to see this French woman-athlete dare to casually sip brandy between sets.

Lenglen dominated women's tennis singles at the 1920 Summer Olympics in Belgium. On her way to winning a gold medal, she lost only four games, three of them in the final against Dorothy Holman of England. She won another gold medal in the mixed doubles event; in the women's doubles, she was eliminated in the semifinals but won bronze after the opposing pair withdrew. At Wimbledon, she won the singles championship every year from 1919 to 1925—except in 1924, when health problems forced her to withdraw after winning the quarterfinal. After 1925, no other Frenchwoman would win the Wimbledon ladies' singles title again until Amélie Mauresmo in 2006. From 1920 to 1926, Lenglen won the French Championships singles title six times and the doubles title five times, as well as three World Hard Court Championships in 1921–1923. Astoundingly, she only lost seven matches in her entire career.

Suzanne Lenglen was the first major female tennis star ever to go pro. Sports promoter C. C. Pyle paid her fifty thousand dollars to tour the US and play a series of matches against Mary K. Browne, who at thirty-five was considered past her best years for tennis—although Browne had made it to the French Championships final that year, she lost to Lenglen and only managed to score one point during the entire match. This was the first time ever that a women's match was the headliner event of such a tour, even though male players were part of the exhibition as well. When the tour ended in early 1927, Lenglen had won every one of her thirty-eight matches; but she was exhausted, and her doctor advised a lengthy respite from the sport. She decided to retire from competition and set up a tennis school with help and funding from her lover, Jean Tillier. The school gradually grew and gained recognition; Lenglen also wrote several tennis texts in those years.

Lenglen's talent, verve, and style had changed women's tennis forever. Before the arc of her brilliant career, very few tennis fans were interested in women's matches. She was inducted into the International Tennis Hall of Fame in 1978, and many hold her to be one of the best tennis players ever. The following year, the French Open began to award a trophy called the "Coupe Suzanne Lenglen" to the winner of the women's singles competition. With this trophy, Suzanne Lenglen's legacy is literally being handed down from champion to champion, as the world watches the skill, athleticism, and excitement of women's tennis.

▲▲▲▲▲▲▲▲▲▲▲▲▲▲▲▲▲▲▲▲▲▲▲▲▲▲▲▲▲▲▲▲▲▲▲▲▲

I belong to that group of people who move the piano by themselves.

—**Eleanor Robson Belmont**, an actress and opera singer who, upon marrying a millionaire, threw herself into charity and art; as a Red Cross representative during World War I, she braved the danger of German U-boats to cross the Atlantic and inspect US Army camps based in Europe

➤➤➤ *Affirmation Station* ◄ ◄◄

I can do anything.

I speak my mind.

I am intelligent.

You have to be taught to be second class; you're not born that way.

—**Lena Horne**, a singer, actress, and civil rights activist who turned down any roles that stereotyped African American women, despite the controversy which her more-than-reasonable refusals caused at the time; she succeeded by finding other, more dignified roles and through her singing career

In southern Spain, they made me eat a bull's testicles. They were really garlicky, which I don't like. I prefer to take a bull by the horns.

—**Padma Lakshmi**, food expert, actress, model, businesswoman, Emmy-nominated TV show host, and *New York Times* bestselling author; her unprecedented career has taken her around the world

After me there are no more jazz singers.

—**Betty Carter**, a jazz singer known for her creative improvisation; she was practically the living embodiment of the saying "My way or the highway," refusing to drop her own interpretation of jazz to produce more mainstream music

Women need not always keep their mouths shut and their wombs open.

—**Emma Goldman**, a writer and activist who refused to allow her opponents to keep her silent, protesting war and advocating for women's rights

▼▼▼▼▼▼▼▼▼▼▼▼▼▼▼▼▼▼▼▼▼▼▼▼▼▼▼▼▼▼▼▼▼▼▼▼

Badass to the Bone:

Emma Goldman

Teenage immigrant Emma Goldman had escaped from Russia in 1885, after witnessing the wholesale slaughter of idealist political rebel anarchists who called themselves the Nihilists. The following year, this young woman, who seemed "born to ride the whirlwinds," learned that America was not immune to political violence. Across the country, anarchists were joining socialists and others in agitating for stronger labor laws to protect workers, including an eight-hour workday. In Chicago, May Day 1886 brought tensions to a boil; on May 3, police opened fire on a crowd of strikers at a factory, killing at least two. The following day, anarchists held a demonstration in Haymarket Square which started out peacefully, but when the police ordered the protestors to disperse, someone threw a bomb and police cleared the square with gunfire. Anarchists were blamed and arrested, Chicago's power elite cracked down on labor and immigrant groups, and the press flew into a hysteria against anarchism. Amid this swirl of popular prejudice, a hostile judge presided over a trial that condemned seven anarchists to death.

The Haymarket affair, rather than scare her away from the politics of idealism forever, drew young Emma further toward the kind of political passion that risked death for principles. She "devoured every line on anarchism I could get," as she notes in her autobiography, *Living My Life*, "and headed for New York City, command central in the 1890s for radicals of many stripes."

In New York, Emma met one of the anarchists whose writing she'd been devouring, Johann Most, who encouraged her to develop her gift for public speaking. Emma worked as a practical nurse in New York's ghettos, where she saw the price women paid for want of any birth control. Soon she was taking to the soapbox to air her views on this lack of available contraception and the resulting reliance on back-alley abortions. Her campaign reached the ears of Margaret Sanger and influenced the development of a national birth control campaign.

She continued to mesmerize crowds with her impassioned speeches until 1917, when her opposition to World War I led to a two-year imprisonment. She was subsequently deported, since the Justice Department was fearful of allowing her to continue her antiwar campaign: "She is womanly, a remarkable orator, tremendously sincere, and carries conviction. If she is allowed to continue here she cannot help but have great influence."

She continued to exercise influence from abroad and in 1922, *The Nation* magazine named her one of "the twelve greatest living women." She was allowed back into the country—after her death, when the government apparently felt that her silenced corpse would pose no risk to the American way of life—and she was buried in Chicago, alongside the Haymarket martyrs.

▲▲

When I fight, there is usually a funeral and it isn't mine.

—**Henrietta Gree**n, the wealthiest American woman of her
   time; after inheriting about ten million dollars from her father

and aunt, she worked on Wall Street and as a moneylender to grow her already considerable fortune—not that you could tell from her thrifty lifestyle

I'm as strong as a man. Girls attract less attention in the frontier zone than men.

—**Andrée de Jongh**, code name Dédée (which means "little mother"), a member of the WWII Belgian Resistance who was awarded the Medal of Freedom with Golden Palm for leading more than a hundred Allied soldiers across occupied France to safety in Spain

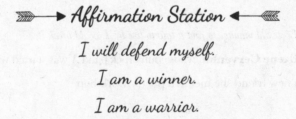

Affirmation Station

I will defend myself.
I am a winner.
I am a warrior.

We are not interested in the possibilities of defeat. They do not exist.

—**Victoria**, Queen of England and Britain's second-longest reigning monarch (outlasted only by Queen Elizabeth II), who spearheaded England's Victorian Era with her stringent personality, morals, and ethics

Please give me some good advice in your next letter. I promise not to follow it.

—Edna St. Vincent Millay, a poet and playwright who made waves with her focus on female sexuality and feminism

Passivity and quietism are invitations to war.

—Dorothy Thompson, the First Lady of American Journalism, whose syndicated column "On the Record" was read by millions of people nationwide

If I ever did manage to find a law to live by, I would break it.

—Exene Cervenka, whose punk rock band *X* was started with a new friend she met at a poetry workshop

The question is not whether we will die, but how we will live.

—Dr. Joan Borysenko, physician, cofounder of a Mind/Body Clinic associated with Harvard Medical School, and *New York Times* bestselling author

>>>→ *Affirmation Station* ←≪≪

I will follow my gut.
I will do things my way.
I fight for my beliefs.

If you send up a weathervane or put your thumb up in the air every time you want to do something different, to find out what people are going to think about it, you're going to limit yourself. That's a very strange way to live.

—**Jessye Norman**, an international opera singer with an exceptional vocal range; she was winner of the 1968 International Music Competition of the German Broadcasting Corporation

It is not easy to find happiness in ourselves, and it is not possible to find it elsewhere.

—**Agnes Repplier**, an essayist and biographer with a sixty-five-year writing career; she had so much trouble learning how to read from her mother that, when she was ten, she finally taught herself

You carry forever the fingerprint that comes from being under someone's thumb.

—**Nancy Banks-Smith**, a British radio and television critic who was recommended for (and turned down!) the Order of the British Empire

You can cry, but don't let it stop you. Don't cry in one spot—cry as you continue to move.

—**Kina**, a famous YouTuber, singer, and songwriter who won the "Doritos Crash the Super Bowl" musical competition

Hope begins in the dark, the stubborn hope that if you just show up and try to do the right thing, the dawn will come. You wait and watch and work: you don't give up.

—**Anne Lamott**, an author of novels and nonfiction works focused on family and real (or realistic, in the case of her fiction) people

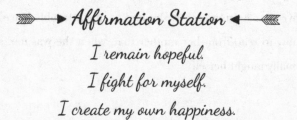

>>> ➤ *Affirmation Station* ◀ ≪

I remain hopeful.
I fight for myself.
I create my own happiness.

The first and worst of all frauds is to cheat one's self. All sin is easy after that.

—**Pearl Bailey**, a United Nations advisor who started out as a Tony Award-winning Broadway actress and singer

A woman [who] is willing to be herself and pursue her own potential runs not so much the risk of loneliness as the challenge of exposure to more interesting men—and people in general.

—**Lorraine Hansberry**, a writer who broke multiple records as both the youngest and the first African American playwright to win a New York Critics' Circle award after writing her play *A Raisin in the Sun*

It requires philosophy and heroism to rise above the opinion of the wise men of all nations and races.

—**Elizabeth Cady Stanton**, an abolitionist and leader of the women's rights movement who helped organize the National Women's Suffrage Association and penned the revolutionary "Declaration of Sentiments"

▼▼▼▼▼▼▼▼▼▼▼▼▼▼▼▼▼▼▼▼▼▼▼▼▼▼▼▼▼▼▼▼▼

Badass to the Bone:

Elizabeth Cady Stanton

In 1869, Susan B. Anthony and Elizabeth Cady Stanton organized the National Women's Suffrage Association and put out a pro-feminist paper, *The Revolution*.

When the Fourteenth Amendment to the Constitution was passed in 1872, guaranteeing all Americans "equal protection of the laws" and specifically protecting the voting rights of "any of the male inhabitants" of any state, Anthony and Cady Stanton kicked into action demanding the right to vote for women as well. They began to work for a separate amendment giving this right to women; however, Congress blithely ignored the amendments put before them each year on the vote for women, and women's suffrage would not come until almost fifty years later.

Both Stanton and Anthony were real hell-raisers. Stanton, along with Lucretia Mott, organized the first women's rights convention in 1848, with a platform on women's rights to property, equal pay for equal work, and the right to vote. Stanton was introduced to Susan B. Anthony three years later. They were a "dream team," combining Elizabeth's political theories and her ability to rouse people's emotions with Susan's unmatched skill as a logician and organizer par excellence. They founded the first temperance society for women and amazed everybody with their drastic call for drunkenness to be recognized as a legal basis for divorce.

Although Elizabeth Cady Stanton would not live to realize her dream of voting rights for women, the successors she trained did finally win this landmark victory for the women of America. Of the 260 women who attended the foremothers' historic first women's rights convention in 1848, only one woman lived long enough to see the passing of the victorious 1920 amendment grating women the right to vote—Charlotte Woodward.

▲▲▲▲▲▲▲▲▲▲▲▲▲▲▲▲▲▲▲▲▲▲▲▲▲▲▲▲▲▲▲▲▲▲▲▲▲▲▲

I am my own Universe; I am my own Professor.

—**Sylvia Ashton-Warner**, an educator and artist who adapted British teaching methods for use with Maori children in New Zealand; she then drew on this experience of merging two vastly different cultures for her personal writing and poetry

Some feminists feel that a woman should never be wrong. We have a right to be wrong.

—**Alice Childress**, an award-winning playwright, novelist, and Tony-nominated actress who started writing after seeing how few good roles there were for African American women in theater

⟫⟫⟫ ➤ *Affirmation Station* ◄ ⟪⟪

I rise above hardships.

I take care of myself.

I am satisfied with my accomplishments.

I look back on my life like a good day's work, it was done and I am satisfied with it.

—**Grandma Moses** (Anna Mary Robertson Moses), a farmer whose detailed, colorful, rustic paintings were displayed at New York City's Museum of Modern Art and around the country

I have often wished I had time to cultivate modesty … but I am too busy thinking about myself.

—**Edith Sitwell**, the legendary writer who, when asked at the age of four about her aspirations for her future, said that she wanted to be a genius when she grew up

By whom?

—**Dorothy Parker**, sassy satirist, critic, poet, and Academy Award-nominated writer, on being told that she was "outspoken"

My mother always told me I wouldn't amount to anything because I procrastinate. I said, "Just wait."

—**Judy Tenuta**, the first standup comic to win the American Comedy Award for "Best Female Comedian"

Did you hear what I said? It was very profound.

—**Dr. Laura Schlessinger**, an advice guru and longtime radio personality whose accomplishments range from hosting her decades-long talk show to becoming, in 1997, the first female winner of the Marconi Award for Network/Syndicated Personality; in 2012, she launched a seasonal line of jewelry, tote bags, and glass and clay art to support the Children of Fallen Patriots Foundation

These women are not any more capable than you are. In fact, they are not any more *anything* than you are. You are just as creative, just as smart, just as powerful. Read these quotes not to put yourself down, but to lift yourself up. To remind yourself what women are capable of—what *you* are capable of. And to remind yourself that it's okay to be confident. In fact, it's *good* to be confident. And you deserve to be.

No matter what you have to do today, no matter what your future holds, you are a strong, independent, beautiful woman, and when you continue to remind yourself of that, you will achieve more than you can even imagine.

Chapter Two

All's Fair in Love and Lust

I think it's fair to say that each and every woman has her own individual ideas on what a romantic relationship is supposed to look like. Should your date knock on the door or honk their car horn to pick you up? Or would you rather meet them at the bar, either for the first time or the hundredth? And don't even get me started on when it's okay to start spending the night—there has never been and never will be an overarching consensus on the "right" way to act when it comes to romance and relationships.

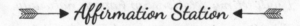

Affirmation Station

I am naturally romantic and polite.
I will not hide who I am.
I let go of all expectations for my love life.

Whether it's love at first sight or a one-night stand, I'm here for you—and so are at least a few of the people quoted below. One of the best parts about dating is that there are no *real* rules—everyone does their own thing, and as long as the people involved are on the same page, no preference is better than another. Want to have sex with a different person every night? Go for it. Waiting 'til marriage? Find a partner who will wait with you or enjoy the single life until you do. Fiercely independent woman who doesn't want a man? We're here for you. No matter what you want, chase after it—though I might advise that you try to avoid the already-married type—and don't let anyone tell you that you're wrong. If your partner likes you, and you like you, you're good.

⟫⟫—▶ *Affirmation Station* ◀—⟪

I realize that a date is potential, not permanent.
I will let my relationship happen naturally.
I will recover from every dating hardship.

But don't fret if you don't seem to be having any luck in the love department. Look below and you'll see that you aren't the only one for whom love isn't always an open door. It's okay to be sad after a breakup and cocoon for a few days, eating only chocolate-flavored foods and watching sappy romance movies that make you cry. Take your time; allow yourself to recover. Once you're done, get back on your feet and move forward. Live your life again. Don't worry about finding your special someone, if that's what you want—and if you'd rather thrive alone, don't worry about ignoring those who may want you to have a "special someone." In fact, maybe just leave worrying behind. Ultimately, what matters is that you're beautiful, loveable, and worthy of attention. The only person who needs to tell you that is you.

Sex is an emotion in motion.

—**Mae West**, an actress, playwright, and burlesque performer who was arrested for her then-scandalous Broadway show *Sex*, which she wrote, directed, and produced herself

Love is our response to our highest values—and can be nothing else.

—**Ayn Rand**, a screenplay writer and author who taught herself to read at the age of six and decided she'd be a writer three years later

Love, by its very nature, is unworldly, and it is for this reason rather than its rarity that it is not only apolitical but antipolitical, perhaps the most powerful of all antipolitical forces.

—**Hannah Arendt**, a twentieth-century political philosopher who famously described "the banality of evil" in her reporting on the 1961 trial of Nazi war criminal Adolf Eichmann

▼▼▼▼▼▼▼▼▼▼▼▼▼▼▼▼▼▼▼▼▼▼▼▼▼▼▼▼▼▼▼▼▼▼▼▼

Badass to the Bone:

Hannah Arendt

German-born Hannah Arendt was a political theorist and philosopher who climbed out of the ivory tower to take direct action against the spread of Fascism. In 1929, at the ripe old age of twenty-two, this brilliant student of theology and Greek earned her PhD from the University of Heidelberg. After a brief arrest by the Gestapo (she was Jewish), she fled to Paris, where she worked for a Zionist resistance organization that sent Jewish orphans to Palestine in hopes of creating a new, united Arab-Jewish nation.

By 1940, she had fled to New York, where she lived among other immigrants and worked for the Council on Jewish Relations and as an editor for Schocken Books; she also served among the leadership of the Jewish Cultural Reconstruction, which, after the war, recovered Jewish writings that had been dispersed by the Nazis. With her first book, *The Origins of Totalitarianism*, she pointed out the common elements in Nazi and Stalinist philosophies and examined the history of European anti-Semitism and "scientific racism." Her subsequent books included *On Revolution*, *The Human*

Condition, and *Thinking and Writing*, as well as her famous discussion of the trial of a Nazi war criminal, *Eichmann in Jerusalem: A Report on the Banality of Evil*, and countless articles and commentaries on such far-reaching subjects as Watergate, Vietnam, and her famous attack on Bertolt Brecht for his "Hymn to Stalin." The first woman to become a full professor at Princeton, she also taught at various other institutions and translated and edited the works of Franz Kafka.

A serious thinker, Arendt became a very public and controversial figure with her beliefs that revolution and war were the central forces of the twentieth century; that there was little organized resistance on the part of the Jews in Europe; and that the Nazi perpetrators were not monsters, but pragmatic rational people accepting evil commands in a banal manner.

Arendt's contributions to the intellectual community are beyond calculation. She made an insular forties America and post-war world look deeply at all the possible causes of the Holocaust. According to his article in *Makers of Nineteenth Century Culture*, Bernard Crick credits Hannah Arendt with "rescu[ing] American intellectuals from an excessive parochiality."

▲▲

The best and most beautiful things in this world cannot be seen or even heard, but must be felt with the heart.

—**Helen Keller**, an inspirational deaf and blind humanitarian who fought for the rights of people with disabilities and for women's rights

I'm a human being and I fall in love, and sometimes I don't have control of every situation.

—**Beyoncé**, a singer whose pop anthems empower women around the world; she garnered fame as part of the R&B group Destiny's Child before becoming a highly successful solo artist, twice performing the Super Bowl halftime show, and making important contributions to the Black Lives Matter movement and the Ban Bossy campaign

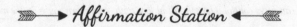

⋙⟶ *Affirmation Station* ⟵⋘

I love and respect my partner.
I will continue to develop a healthy relationship
with my partner.
I will allow love to find me.

Love isn't something you find. Love is something that finds you.

—**Loretta Young**, an Oscar-winning actress who started making her total of nearly one hundred films before she turned five years old

Love always ends differently and it always begins differently.

—**Taylor Swift**, country singer turned pop sensation; her infamous breakups have fueled many a successful song lyric

It is a curious thought, but it is only when you see people looking ridiculous that you realize just how much you love them.

—**Agatha Christie**, a mystery author, romance writer, and playwright whose works have sold billions of copies worldwide

You can never control who you fall in love with, even when you're in the most sad, confused time of your life. You don't fall in love with people because they're fun. It just happens.

—**Kirsten Dunst**, a German-American actress who started modeling and acting at the age of three

It was never just sex. … It was about connection. It was about looking at another human being and seeing your own loneliness and neediness reflected back. It was recognizing that together you had the power to temporarily banish that sense of isolation. It was about experiencing what it was to be human at the basest, most instinctive level. How could that be described as just anything?

—**Emily Maguire**, a singer who coped with her very painful fibromyalgia and difficult mental disorders by writing music and living on a self-sustaining farm with a friend

Affirmation Station

*I will communicate clearly and kindly
with my partner.
I deserve a healthy relationship.
I will always be myself.*

I love a man with a great sense of humor and who is intelligent—a man who has a great smile. He has to make me laugh. I like a man who is very ambitious and driven and who has a good heart and makes me feel safe. I

like a man who is very strong and independent and confident … but at the same time, he's very kind to people.

—**Nicole Scherzinger**, internationally renowned singer and judge on *The X Factor*; she got her own big break by winning on *Popstars*, the predecessor to *American Idol*, and now she is able to help other new talent find their own voice

Love is friendship that has caught fire. It is quiet understanding, mutual confidence, sharing and forgiving. It is loyalty through good and bad times. It settles for less than perfection and makes allowances for human weaknesses.

—**Ann Landers**, an advice columnist, nationally famous for her wit and straightforward words of wisdom, who wrote "Ask Ann Landers" daily for forty-seven years; her sister wrote "Dear Abby," a rival advice column

When you forgive, you heal your own anger and hurt and are able to let love lead again. It's like spring cleaning for your heart.

—**Marci Shimoff**, a writer whose *New York Times* bestselling self-help book series *Chicken Soup for the Soul* has been translated into thirty-three languages

You don't love someone because they're perfect, you love them in spite of the fact that they're not.

—**Jodi Picoult**, a feminist screenwriter, editor, technical writer, novelist, and teacher whose work covers everything from the Holocaust to gun control to teen suicide

I saw that you were perfect, and so I loved you. Then I saw that you were not perfect and I loved you even more.

—**Angelita Lim**, a woman whose famous quote has been reprinted on everything from pillows to picture frames

⟩⟩⟩ → *Affirmation Station* ← ⟨⟨⟨

I am willing to compromise with my partner.
I will not allow my partner to devalue me.
I naturally shift my focus away from looks.

We all have a childhood dream that when there is love, everything goes like silk, but the reality is that marriage requires a lot of compromise.

—**Raquel Welch**, an actress and singer who was thrust into the world of fame as a sex symbol after her work on *One Million Years B.C.*

When you love someone, all your saved-up wishes start coming out.

—**Elizabeth Bowen**, a writer whose novels and short stories often follow unprepared girls through their lives and unhappy relationships as members of the upper-middle-class

If we lose love and self-respect for each other, this is how we finally die.

—**Maya Angelou**, poet, singer, memoirist and civil rights activist; her many accomplishments included more than fifty honorary doctorates and multiple international bestsellers

▼▼▼▼▼▼▼▼▼▼▼▼▼▼▼▼▼▼▼▼▼▼▼▼▼▼▼▼▼▼▼▼▼▼

Badass to the Bone:

Maya Angelou

Marguerite Johnson's childhood was marked by the hardship of the Depression years in which she grew up. Her parents divorced and packed her off to live with her granny, "Momma" Henderson, who eked out a living in Stamps, Arkansas, running a little general store. When she visited her mother in St. Louis, tragedy struck. Her mother had a boyfriend who spent a lot of time at her mother's house and often touched and hugged the seven-year-old overly much, but, in her innocence, she mistook it for a father's love. Later, he raped her, and Maya felt guilty and responsible for his jailing and subsequent death at the hands of other inmates who exacted their own brand of justice on a child molester. She became catatonic as a result of this onslaught of catastrophic violence. With the support of her family and an adult friend, Bertha Flowers, who introduced her to literature, Maya gradually reentered the world.

Maya and her mother then moved to San Francisco, where her mother ran a boardinghouse and worked as a professional gambler. Maya met many colorful characters among the boarders and threw herself into school, where she flourished. She got pregnant at sixteen and took on the full responsibilities of motherhood with the birth of her son, Guy. For a few years, Maya walked on the wild side: working at a Creole restaurant, waitressing at a bar in San Diego, even spending an accidental and brief stint as a madam for two lesbian prostitutes. ... Maya started singing and dancing at the Purple Onion, where she took the name "Maya Angelou," and broke into show biz as part of the road show for *Porgy and Bess*, touring Africa and Europe. After cowriting *Cabaret for Freedom* with Godfrey Cambridge for the Southern Christian Leadership Conference, Maya drew Martin Luther King, Jr.'s attention for her talent and contribution to the civil rights movement, and he invited her to serve as an SCLC coordinator.

Maya's career was absolutely astonishing after this point. She lived in Egypt with Guy and her lover, a South African freedom fighter, and worked in Ghana writing for *The African Review*. She remained involved with the theater, writing and performing in plays, acting in *Roots*, and writing several volumes of poetry as well as the script and music for the movie of her autobiography. But it is for the six bestselling volumes of her autobiography, starting with *I Know Why the Caged Bird Sings*, that she will go down in literary history. Written with captivating honesty, color, and verve, they are read by youth and adults alike for their inspirational message.

▲▲▲▲▲▲▲▲▲▲▲▲▲▲▲▲▲▲▲▲▲▲▲▲▲▲▲▲▲▲▲▲▲▲▲▲▲▲

Sex is like washing your face—just something you do because you have to. Sex without love is absolutely ridiculous. Sex follows love, it never precedes it.
—**Sophia Loren**, an actress who worked hard to push herself up and out of a difficult and poor childhood to be a highly successful Academy Award-winning star

I need sex for a clear complexion, but I'd rather do it for love.

—**Joan Crawford**, an actress who successfully reinvented herself every decade to reach and maintain Hollywood stardom

Really, sex and laughter do go very well together, and I wondered—and I still do—which is more important.

—**Hermione Gingold**, an actress whose love life was almost as popular as her stage and screen performances

➤➤➤ *Affirmation Station* ◄ ◄◄

I am a confident and capable lover.
I am a powerful sexual being.
I will have sex only when I want to.

For women, the best aphrodisiacs are words. The G-spot is in the ears. He who looks for it below there is wasting his time.

—**Isabel Allende**, a writer whose internationally renowned books have sold over sixty-seven million copies in more than thirty-five languages

The eyes are one of the most powerful tools a woman can have. With one look, she can relay the most intimate message. After the connection is made, words cease to exist.

—**Jennifer Salaiz**, a writer who flourished in the erotica genre after she found that her romance writings were a bit too detailed for younger audiences

A relationship is a relationship that has to be earned, not to be compromised for. And I love relationships; I think they're fantastically wonderful, I think they're great. I think there's nothing in the world more beautiful than falling in love. But falling in love for the right reason. Falling in love for the right purpose. When you fall in love, what is there to compromise about?

—**Eartha Kitt**, the first singer of "Santa Baby" and one of the first actresses to play Catwoman

The easiest kind of relationship is with ten thousand people, the hardest is with one.

—**Joan Baez**, a folk singer whose topical music promoted pacifism, social justice, and civil rights

▼▼▼▼▼▼▼▼▼▼▼▼▼▼▼▼▼▼▼▼▼▼▼▼▼▼▼▼▼▼▼▼▼▼▼

Badass to the Bone:

Joan Baez

Folk shero and guitarist Joan Baez tapped her muse young—as a college student at Boston University. In 1960, at age nineteen, she became a household name overnight with her first album, *Joan Baez*. Fiercely political, her recordings such as "We Shall Overcome" point to her alignment with civil rights, and she was one of the best known Vietnam War protestors and worked for the No Nukes campaign as well. Oddly enough, one of the causes Joan never aligned herself with was feminism. "I don't relate with feminism. I see the whole human race as being broken and terribly in need, not just women." With her inspirational voice and her long dark hair, she gave a generation of women a model of activism, personal freedom, and self-determination. Baez lives by her own light—and in so doing, encourages us all to follow our consciences.

▲▲▲▲▲▲▲▲▲▲▲▲▲▲▲▲▲▲▲▲▲▲▲▲▲▲▲▲▲▲▲▲▲▲▲

Pleasure of love lasts but a moment. Pain of love lasts a lifetime.

—**Bette Davis**, an actress whose larger-than-life persona came through in each of her nearly one hundred roles on the silver screen

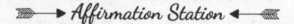

Affirmation Station

I am happy being single and independent.

I have a lot of fun when I'm single.

I deserve to be appreciated.

I don't think marriages break up because of what you do to each other. They break up because of what you must become in order to stay in them.

—**Carol Grace**, an actress and author who is the self-proclaimed inspiration for the *Breakfast at Tiffany's* novella's protagonist, Holly Golightly

A successful marriage requires falling in love many times, always with the same person.

—**Mignon McLaughlin**, an editor, playwright, and writer whose short stories touched the heart of many a magazine-reader

When you find your soulmate, you could sleep under their armpits.

—**Heather Mills**, a model who quit that glamorous career in favor of activism when her leg was amputated after being hit by a police motorcycle

A gentleman holds my hand.
A man pulls my hair.
A soulmate will do both.

—**Alessandra Torre**, a *New York Times* bestselling author whose adult romance and suspense novels have graced many an e-book shelf

If sex is such a natural phenomenon, how come there are so many books on how to do it?

—**Bette Midler**, an actress and singer whose New York Restoration Project has planted over a million trees in low-income neighborhoods of New York City

⟫⟫ ➤ *Affirmation Station* ◀ ⟪⟪

I will show my appreciation for my partner.
I am a unique lover and partner.
I will value my partner's one-of-a-kind
positive traits.

There are as many kinds of kisses as there are people on earth, as there are permutations and combinations of those people. No two people kiss alike—no two people f*** alike—but somehow the kiss is more personal, more individualized than the f***.

—**Diane di Prima**, a teacher who cofounded the San Francisco Institute of Magical and Healing Arts

Sexiness is all in the eye of the beholder. I think it should be. Absolutely. My sex appeal, whatever it might be, isn't obvious … at least to me.

—**Sharon Tate**, a model and actress who was infamously murdered by Charles Manson cult followers before she was even thirty years old

I'm kind of a good girl—and I'm not. I'm a good girl because I really believe in love, integrity, and respect. I'm a bad girl because I like to tease. I know that I have sex appeal in my deck of cards.

—**Katy Perry**, a singer whose highly lucrative pop songs range in content from sex anthems to songs with politically-tinted choruses

I know of my sex appeal. I know about sexuality, and I know how to use it—tastefully, of course.

—**Rachel Bilson**, an actress who made a name for herself after she was encouraged by her father to pursue acting upon dropping out of college

A historical romance is the only kind of book where chastity really counts.

—**Barbara Cartland**, a prolific writer who just happened to be the step-grandmother of Princess Diana; she who wrote a whopping seven hundred books during her lifetime

⇒→ Affirmation Station ←⇐

I am overcoming my sexual insecurities.
I provide immense sexual pleasure to my partner.
Feeling sexually confident is a natural part
of my life.

Love is so much better when you are not married.

—**Maria Callas**, an internationally acclaimed opera singer
with an impressive and captivating vocal range

I need more sex, OK? Before I die, I wanna taste everyone in the world.

—**Angelina Jolie**, an actress and UN Refugee Agency Goodwill
Ambassador; her twelve-year relationship with actor Brad Pitt,
which led to a brief marriage, was dubbed "Brangelina" and
was followed almost as closely as her movie career

I do quite naughty things now. I do like to be a bit sexy.

—**Kylie Minogue**, a superstar whose accidental music career
led to a history-making winning streak of more than twenty
consecutive top-ten hits in the United Kingdom

Sick and perverted always appeals to me.

—**Madonna**, a singer, actor, and music producer whose hard work and constant image reinvention led to her becoming the world's richest female musician in 2008

▼▼▼▼▼▼▼▼▼▼▼▼▼▼▼▼▼▼▼▼▼▼▼▼▼▼▼▼▼▼▼▼▼

Badass to the Bone:

Madonna

Has there been anyone in American culture who has remade herself as often—or as well—as Madonna? As an artist, her own physical form and public image have served as much a canvas for Madonna as her music has, and her many incarnations almost seem like different women's lives. And in each of them, Madonna has evoked controversy.

She's been a target for her open approach to sex and the presence of eroticism in her work. Her sheroism as a gay rights and AIDS activist received much less press than her pointy bras did. Madonna was threatened with jail on several occasions for her pro-gay stance; she took the challenge and remained steadfast in her solidarity with the gay community.

Madonna Louise Veronica Ciccone was born into a staunchly Catholic home in Michigan in 1958. Her mother was extremely puritanical; before she died (when Madonna was six), she taught her daughter that pants that zip up the front were sinful. By the time Madonna was a teen, she had fame on the brain and escaped to New York City as soon as possible to make it happen. Struggling as a dancer, she lived as a squatter until she hit the big time with "Lucky Star" in 1984. Since then, she has sold more than one hundred million records, has appeared in fifteen films, had dozens of top-ten hits, and penned a very controversial book entitled *Sex*.

Beautiful, powerful, and unflinchingly honest, motherhood suits Madonna well—and she has also flourished as a businesswoman with her successful label, Maverick Records. After her highly praised performance as Evita in the musical drama of the same name, Madonna no longer has to prove herself in any arena and is relaxed, confident, and grounded. She is also more vibrant than ever, looking back over her Manhattan days as a starving squatter, her hard-earned stardom and musing at the changes daughter Lourdes Maria Ciccone Leon and son

Rocco John Ritchie brought to her life. She has adopted several children and has recently been a voice for the Trump Resistance.

▲▲▲

A woman without a man is like a fish without a bicycle.

—**Gloria Steinem**, an activist and writer who founded the Ms. Foundation for Women and cofounded, among other things, the National Women's Political Caucus, the Women's Action Alliance, *Ms.* Magazine, and URGE

▼▼▼▼▼▼▼▼▼▼▼▼▼▼▼▼▼▼▼▼▼▼▼▼▼▼▼▼▼▼▼▼▼▼▼▼▼▼▼

Badass to the Bone:

Gloria Steinem

Gloria Steinem's name is synonymous with feminism. As a leader of the Second Wave of feminism, she brought a new concern to the fore—the importance of self-esteem for women. Her childhood did little to bolster her sense of self or predict the successful course her life would take. Escaping through books and movies, Gloria did well at school and eventually was accepted to Smith College, where her interest in women's rights, sparked by her awareness that her mother's illness had not been taken seriously because "her functioning was not necessary to the world," began to take hold.

After a junket in India, she started freelancing; her goal was to be a political reporter. Soon she hit the glass ceiling; while she made enough money to get by, she wasn't getting the kind of serious assignments her male colleagues were—interviewing Presidential candidates and writing on foreign policy. Instead she was assigned in 1963 to go undercover as a Playboy Bunny and write about it. She agreed, seeing it as an investigative journalism piece, a way to expose sexual harassment. However, after the story appeared, no editors would take her seriously; she was the girl who had worked as a Bunny.

But she kept pushing for political assignments and finally, in 1968, came on board the newly founded *New York* magazine as a contributing editor. When the magazine sent her to cover a radical feminist meeting, no one guessed the assignment would be transformational. After attending the meeting, she moved from the sidelines to stage center of the feminist movement, cofounding the National Women's Political Caucus and the Women's Action Alliance.

The next year, Steinem, with her background in journalism, was the impetus for the founding of *Ms.*, the first mainstream feminist magazine in America's history. The first issue, with shero Wonder Woman on the cover, sold out the entire first printing of three hundred thousand in an unprecedented eight days, and *Ms.* received an astonishing twenty thousand letters soon after the magazine hit the newsstands, indicating it had really struck a chord with the women of America.

The self-described "itinerant speaker and feminist organizer" continued at the helm of *Ms.* for fifteen years, publishing articles such as the one that posited Marilyn Monroe as the embodiment of fifties women's struggle to keep up the expectations of society.

Gloria Steinem's real genius lies in her ability to relate to other women, creating the bond of sisterhood with shared feelings; this comes through in her heralded memoir. Still a phenomenally popular speaker and writer, Gloria Steinem crystallizes the seemingly complicated issues and challenges of her work by defining feminism as simply, "the belief that women are full human beings."

▲▲

Lift your hips for me, love.

—**Tahereh Mafi**, a bestselling author who had so many people ask her how to say her name that she posted a recording of the correct pronunciation on her website

No matter what stage you're at in your love life, you deserve to be treated with kindness and respect. You deserve to be able to make your own timeline for finding or getting to know your lover, whether they're your one true love or just the person who's making you happy at the moment. And you don't have to prove yourself—or defend your choices—to anyone. This is your love life, and the only one who needs to understand how you live it is you.

Chapter Three

Stay Beautiful, Inside and Out

Contrary to often-popular belief, there is no right way to be beautiful. Culture's definition of beauty has changed greatly even in just the past fifty years, and it will change even more in the next fifty. What won't change is the fact that you're beautiful. No, don't dismiss that sentence. A certain famous boy band was wrong when they intoned that not knowing you're beautiful is exactly what makes you beautiful. That just isn't true, there's no other way to say it. You're gorgeous, and you deserve to know it.

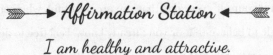

Affirmation Station

I am healthy and attractive.
I am free of negativity.
I see myself as beautiful.

What is beauty? Well, it's certainly not related to whether you have the same body type of the most prominent actress or model of the moment. Don't get me wrong, they're beautiful too. But not because they look a certain way. While beauty may start on the surface, it goes much deeper than that. Beauty is who you are, not what you look like. And whether you have wrinkles or smooth skin, whether you look older or younger than you actually are, whether you have a few extra pounds or you can't seem to gain weight no matter what you eat, you are beautiful.

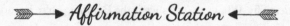

Affirmation Station

I am beautiful on the inside and outside.
I am comfortable with myself.
I think positively.

Remind yourself every day that you are beautiful, whether you struggle to believe that or you already know. Feel free to accept compliments with confidence—even those who strive for modesty need to know that denying the truth does not make you humble, it makes you a liar. You don't have to say "Oh, no, I'm not" to preserve your likeability. And if you really believe that you're not beautiful—if you even believe that you're unattractive or ugly—it's time to change that. So say "Thank you" or "I know" when people compliment you, whatever your preference is, and learn how to be comfortable in your own skin. It may feel weird at first, but you can do it, and you deserve to.

➤➤➤ Affirmation Station ◄ ◄◄

I feel good about myself.
I am comfortable in my own skin.
When I look in the mirror, I see beauty.

Beauty is not perfection. Beauty is not flawlessness. Beauty is not flustered denials or obligation-fueled returned compliments, it's not a certain weight or body shape. Beauty is staying true to yourself and feeling good when you look in the mirror. I'm not saying you aren't allowed to go on a diet or try to lose weight, or that you can't wear makeup or care about current fashion—I just want you to know that you're already beautiful now. You might want those things to be healthier or as something fun to wear or do, and that's great! But you don't need them to be beautiful. Decide now that you will stop telling yourself anything other than the truth, and affirm that truth each and every day. You're a beaut.

The heck with the natural look. Where would Marilyn Monroe be if she clung to the hair color God gave her?

—**Adair Lara**, an award-winning author and teacher with a sense of humor, which she likes to share with the world through her writings

Never "just run out for a few minutes" without looking your best. This is not vanity—it's self-liking.

—**Estée Lauder**, a businesswoman whose cosmetics company was so successful that she became one of the richest women in the world

I think I'm a very pretty girl. I'm never going to pretend to think otherwise.

—**Milla Jovovich**, an actress whose zombie-hunting character in the *Resident Evil* movie series is almost as impressive as the real-life woman who makes that character come to life

I'm tired of all this nonsense about beauty being only skin-deep. That's deep enough. What do you want, an adorable pancreas?

—**Jean Kerr**, a woman of letters whose refusal to give up her passion after the commercial failure of her first plays led to a successful career as an impressive writer

Clothes and courage have much to do with each other.

—**Sara Jeannette Duncan**, a journalist whose world travels inspired many a successful piece of writing

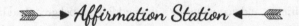 **Affirmation Station**

I am comfortable in my clothes.

I am naturally beautiful.

I recognize that I have true beauty.

I'm a big woman. I need big hair.

—**Aretha Franklin**, a singer who won an impressive eighteen Grammy awards; she was also the Rock and Roll Hall of Fame's first female artist inductee

Badass to the Bone:

Aretha Franklin

A preacher's daughter, Aretha Franklin started her musical career early, appearing with her famous dad, Revered Clarence

LaVaugh Franklin, at Detroit's New Baptist Church. By the age of eight, in 1950, Aretha electrified her father's congregation with her first gospel solo; by fourteen, she'd cut her first gospel record, *Songs of Faith*. Encouraged by her father and his circle of friends and acquaintances, the budding gospel great had her eyes on the glittery prize of pop stardom. She decided to move to New York to pursue her dream in 1960.

The following year she released an album on Columbia Records, *Aretha*, which positioned her as a jazz artist, covering classics like "God Bless the Child," "Ol' Man River," and "Over the Rainbow." Franklin went on to record ten albums with Columbia, while record execs waffled about how to package her. Jerry Wexler of Atlantic Records was a fan of Aretha and signed her immediately when her contract with Columbia ran out. Wexler rightly saw Aretha as an R&B singer. She agreed. Her debut album on Atlantic, *I Never Loved a Man*, contained the hit "Respect," which catapulted Franklin to number one on both the pop and the R&B charts. "Respect" became an anthem in 1967 for both feminists and black activists.

"Respect" was just the beginning of a chain of hits for the singer: "Baby, I Love You," "Natural Woman," and "Chain of Fools" came hot on the heels of the international smash hit, and soon Aretha was dubbed the "Queen of Soul" and reigned over the music world with the power and authority of her God-given gift.

▲▲▲▲▲▲▲▲▲▲▲▲▲▲▲▲▲▲▲▲▲▲▲▲▲▲▲▲▲▲▲▲▲▲▲▲▲▲▲

My idea of sexy is that less is more. The less you reveal, the more people can wonder.

—**Emma Watson**, an actress and UN Women Goodwill Ambassador, best known for playing Hermione Granger in the *Harry Potter* movie series

I see myself as sexy. If you are comfortable with it, it can be very classy and appealing.

—**Aaliyah**, singer and actress who started her career at the age of twelve; her life was cut short by a plane crash only ten years later

To dance confident in fringe panties when you're five-four with cellulite is a great thing.

—**Drew Barrymore**, who overcame addiction and a wild reputation to garner amazing success as an actress, producer, and model

I like to mix the street look with classy and sexy. I call it "hood chic."

—**Justine Skye**, a singer and model whose successful career started young, when she took a risk and lifted her voice; her entertainment lawyer mother had brought her along to a BMI music panel, where she unexpectedly stood up during the Q&A session and asked to for an impromptu audition

>>>→ *Affirmation Station* ←◂◂

I am naturally sexy.
I possess inner beauty.
I am an original.

I went shopping last week looking for feminine protection. I looked at all the products and I decided on a .38 revolver.

—**Karen Ripley**, a standup comic and improviser whose play *Show Me Where It Hurts* won SF Fringe Best Musical Comedy

The fashionable woman is sexy, witty, and dry-cleaned.

—**Mary Quant**, timeless fashion icon and originator of the miniskirt; she opened Bazaar, an affordable retail boutique, so she could share her clothes with younger (and less rich) clients

You can have anything you want in life you dress for it.

—**Edith Head**, whose costumes have won her an astonishing eight Academy Awards

When a photographer shoots a celebrity, they must be taking photos of our inner selves, because I'm always shocked by the way I look … I'm way hotter in my own mind.

—**Pamela Anderson**, animal rights activist, model, and actress of *Playboy* and *Baywatch* fame

Who said that clothes make a statement? What an understatement that was. Clothes never shut up.

—**Susan Brownmiller**, a writer and actress who increased the public's awareness of violent crimes against women and children

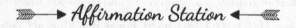

Affirmation Station

I love the way I look.

I am friendly, positive, and outgoing.

I naturally attract others with my charisma.

I put this coat on layaway. It was this brown suede thing and I thought it was fabulous, the ultimate. I had it for about two days when our house got robbed, and it was stolen. … If you see me sobbing in a movie, I'm thinking about that.

—**Julia Roberts**, who pursued acting after deciding she wasn't science-minded enough for veterinarian work and became one of the highest-paid actors in Hollywood

Oh, never mind the fashion. When one has a style of one's own, it is always twenty times better.

—**Margaret Oliphant**, who published over one hundred books to provide for her children, nieces, and nephews

I try to be as unsexy as possible.

—**Dusty Springfield**, a famed singer and Rock and Roll Hall of Fame inductee

I'm not a "sexy" "beautiful" woman. It takes a lot of work to make me look like a girl.

—**Megan Fox**, an actress and model in many "sexiest" lists, such as *FHM* magazine's "Sexiest Woman Alive"

I really don't think I need buns of steel. I'd be happy with buns of cinnamon.

—**Ellen DeGeneres**, beloved comedian and talk show host who holds numerous People's Choice and Emmy awards

⇢➤ *Affirmation Station* ⬅⇠

I believe in myself.
I see myself as confident and successful.
I am transforming into a confident,
beautiful person.

Being sexy is all about attitude, not body type. It's a state of mind.

—**Ameesha Patel**, a winner of awards in both economics and acting, whose overnight acting success led her to leave finance behind in favor of her very successful career in film

It's nice to just embrace the natural beauty within you.

—**Victoria Justice**, who moved from her birthplace in Hollywood, Florida, to Hollywood, California, to pursue acting, which has been her passion since the age of eight

Looking good is almost as important as running well. It's part of feeling good about myself.

—**Florence Griffith-Joyner**, groundbreaking Olympic athlete

▼▼▼▼▼▼▼▼▼▼▼▼▼▼▼▼▼▼▼▼▼▼▼▼▼▼▼▼▼▼▼▼▼▼

Badass to the Bone:

Florence Griffith-Joyner

When Jackie Joyner-Kersee's brother, Al Joyner, met the flamboyant Florence Griffith in 1984, the runner who made her mark on the track world as much for her long fingernails and colorful attire as for being "the world's fastest woman," she was working days as a customer service rep for a bank and moonlighting as a beautician at night. The former world-class runner had lost the gold to Valerie Brisco in 1980 and had given up. At Al's urging, she began training again. They also started dating seriously and got married soon after. This time, Florence had the will to win and stormed the 1988 Seoul Olympics to take home three gold medals. Off the track, "Flo-Jo," as the press dubbed her, has devoted herself to working with children, hoping to educate the youth of America to "reach beyond their dreams," eat right, play sports, and stay away from drugs. After her record-setting gold medal races in Seoul, *Ms.* enthused, "Florence Griffith-Joyner has joined the immortals, rising to their status on the force of her amazing athletic achievement, aided by the singular nature of her personality and approach."

▲▲▲▲▲▲▲▲▲▲▲▲▲▲▲▲▲▲▲▲▲▲▲▲▲▲▲▲▲▲▲▲▲▲▲▲▲▲▲

Character isn't inherited. One builds it daily by the way one thinks and acts, thought by thought, action by action. If one lets fear or hate or anger take possession of the mind, they become self-forged chains.

—**Helen Gahagan Douglas**, whose political career took off after the Great Depression, when she decided to leave acting to work with the Democratic Party

Elegance is the only beauty that never fades.

—**Audrey Hepburn**, the *Breakfast at Tiffany's* star who's won every major kind of acting award, not to mention the Presidential Medal of Freedom

Beauty is when you can appreciate yourself. When you love yourself, that's when you're most beautiful.

—**Zoe Kravitz**, who broke out of the shadow of her parents' music and acting success to garner her own in *X-Men: First Class* and *Fantastic Beasts: The Crimes of Grindelwald*

➤➤➤ ➤ *Affirmation Station* ◀ ◀◀◀

I take care of myself.
I am perfect in my imperfection.
I like my body.

Imperfection is beauty, madness is genius and it's better to be absolutely ridiculous than absolutely boring.

—**Marilyn Monroe**, who took advantage of a chance discovery by a photographer to change her life and build a successful modeling and acting career

Beauty has so many forms, and I think the most beautiful thing is confidence and loving yourself.

—**Kiesza**, who worked as a code breaker in the Royal Canadian Navy before competing in Miss Universe Canada and then moving on to become a singer-songwriter

I love fashion, and I love changing my style, my hair, my makeup, and everything I've done in the past has made me what I am now. Not everyone is going to like what I do, but I look back at everything, and it makes me smile.

—**Victoria Beckham**, a Spice Girls singer and leader of her own fashion empire

For me, style is essentially doing things well. If you want to be outrageous, be outrageous with style. If you want to be restrained, be restrained with style. One can't specifically define style. It's like the perfume to a flower. It's a quality you can't analyze.

—**Françoise Gilot**, who had a highly successful art career despite her angry ex, Picasso, attempting to ruin it

I could clap back and say a few things to you. But instead I'll let your words … speak for themselves. And that will be the last word.

—**Sharon Reed**, an incredible news anchor well-known for her confidence and determination

≫→ *Affirmation Station* ←≪

I take pride in who I am.
I accept myself deeply and completely.
I am immune to negative thinking.

I was admonished to adopt feminine clothes; I refused, and still refuse. As for other avocations for women, there are plenty of other women to perform them.

—**Joan of Arc**, a French war-hero, martyr, and saint who was burned at the stake by the English for wearing armor; the prior year, she had led France to a brilliant victory over England at Orléans

Beauty always promises, but never gives anything.

—**Simone Weil**, whose activism started early when, at the age of five, she refused to eat sugar because she knew that WWI soldiers on the front lines didn't have access to any

You've probably noticed already that I'm dressed like a grown-up. ... I apologize to the Academy, and I promise that I will never do it again.

—**Cher**, an internationally renowned, award-winning actress and singer who became a household name quickly after her career as a performer began

I keep my campaign promises, but I never promised to wear stockings.

—**Ella T. Grasso**, whose long career in politics reached its zenith when she defeated her opponent and became the first female Governor of Connecticut

It's me, and I love me. I learned to love me. I've been like this my whole life, and I embrace me. I love how I look. I love that I'm a full woman and I'm strong and I'm powerful and I'm beautiful at the same time. There's nothing wrong with that.

—**Serena Williams**, a tennis player with multiple Grand Slam titles and Olympic gold medals

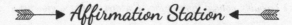

Affirmation Station

I will stop comparing myself to others.
I know that I am a beautiful person.
I am internally validated.

A smile is so sexy, yet so warm. When someone genuinely smiles at you, it's the greatest feeling in the world.

—**Mandy Moore**, a singer and actress known for lending her voice to the animated Disney Princess Rapunzel

There are two ways of spreading light. To be the candle, or the mirror that reflects it.

—**Edith Wharton**, a writer who was the first woman to win the Pulitzer Prize for Fiction, a full membership in the American Academy of Arts and Letters, and an honorary Doctorate of Letters from Yale University

I love thongs. The day they were invented, sunshine broke through the clouds.

—**Sandra Bullock**, an Academy Award-winning actress known for her roles in *The Blind Side* and *Gravity*

A woman's dress should be like a barbed-wire fence: serving its purpose without obstructing the view.

—**Sophia Loren**, who worked hard to rise out of a difficult and poor childhood to become a highly successful, Academy Award-winning actress

I see my body as an instrument, rather than an ornament.

—**Alanis Morissette**, an alternative rock musician who wrote her first song when she was nine, a year before she started acting on Nickelodeon

Honey, I am going to my grave with my eyelashes and my makeup on.

—**Tammy Faye Bakker**, reality TV star, televangelist, talk show host, and author

As you can see, beauty and sexiness mean a lot of different things to a lot of different people. But what doesn't change is the reality that you hold both of those things inside yourself. Those adjectives describe you, even in your pajamas, even before you

take a shower, even if you're honestly just having a rough day and aren't being perfectly poised and polite right now.

You are beautiful. It's important to tell yourself that.

Chapter Four

Do You Work Here?

Women may not have always been paid for their jobs, but they have always had to work, and work *hard*. From the more traditional professions of child-rearing and home-managing to modern jobs like CEO and entrepreneur, women have always known what it is to pull up their proverbial bootstraps and get down-and-dirty. And we've proven time and time again that anything women want to do, we can. Women are directors, bureaucrats, artists, writers, waitresses, teachers, professors, trash collectors, monarchs, executives, activists—the list goes on. If a job exists, there's a woman who can do it *well*.

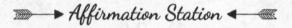

Affirmation Station

People trust my opinions and expertise.
I am a proven leader.
I am a good decision maker.

And women are owning their success, whatever the word means for them. We know that we're good at what we do, and we won't let anyone tell us otherwise. And you know what? You're good at what you do, too. Whether you're still learning how to do your job or you've been doing it for the past fifty years, you can know that you're a capable person who is doing a great job.

Your best is not just good enough, it's what your employers need. You are irreplaceable.

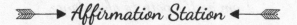

Affirmation Station

I maximize success in all areas of my life.
I push limits and get the most out of life.
I reach higher and further every day.

It doesn't matter what you're doing right now, and it doesn't matter if you think you'll stay where you are for five months or five years. Success is what you make it. If success means you'll be the head of a Fortune 500 company before you retire, do what it takes to get there—and do it without stepping on the unwilling backs of others. If it means raising kids who become extraordinary adults, then take pride in your work as a mother. If it means making a positive difference in the world, then, well, we are all capable of doing that—you just need to figure out how *you're* going to. And if you don't know what success means to you yet, don't fret. Find yourself a position that you don't hate and figure it out along the way.

⟫⟫ ➤ *Affirmation Station* ◄ ⟪

I am highly driven and motivated to succeed.
I am on the path to abundance.
I am creating a wonderful life for myself.

Ultimately, you can do whatever you want (though I might advise against anything with questionable legality, myself). As you grow and change, your definition of success might, too. But no matter what you end up doing with your career, know that you are capable of doing amazing things. You can and will reach your goals. So each morning when you're looking at yourself in the mirror, take a moment to affirm your capability—and to affirm the inevitability of your success.

How we spend our days is of course, how we spend our lives.
—**Annie Dillard**, a Pulitzer Prize-winning author who wanted to use her "rough edges" as a can-opener to escape the world

If I'd been a housemaid I'd have been the best in Australia—I couldn't help it. It's got to be perfection for me.

—**Nellie Melba**, an opera soprano and diva known for her larger-than-life personality and incredible voice

All things are possible until they are proved impossible—and even the impossible may only be so, as of now.

—**Pearl Buck**, a humanitarian and Pulitzer Prize-winning author who was the first female American Nobel laureate, winning the Nobel Prize for Literature

It is necessary to try to pass one's self always; this occupation ought to last as long as life.

—**Christina, Queen of Sweden**, who prevented her country from falling into civil war and voluntarily abdicated her own throne

If you want to stand out don't be different, be outstanding.

—**Meredith West**, an esteemed professor whose research interests include how behavior develops in humans and animals

⟫⟫⟩ → *Affirmation Station* ← ⟨⟪⟪

Nothing is impossible for me.
I have unshakeable dedication to my goals.
I am a highly focused individual.

It's not how fast you get here but how long you stay.

—**Patty Berg**, the Ladies Professional Golf Association's first president and winner of over eighty golf tournaments

If one is going to change things, one has to make a fuss and catch the eye of the world.

—**Elizabeth Janeway**, an author whose highly praised psychological insight and incredible writing led to her being known as a modern Jane Austen

One baby is a patient baby, and waits indefinitely until its mother is ready to feed it. The other baby is an impatient baby and cries lustily, screams and

kicks and makes everybody unpleasant until it is fed. Well, we know perfectly well which baby is attended to first. That is the whole history of politics.

—**Emmeline Pankhurst**, a leader of the British women's suffrage movement and founder of the Women's Social and Political Union

Opportunity knocked. My doorman threw him out.

—**Adrienne Gusoff**, whose lengthy resume includes the roles of author, humor writer, greeting-card writer, and costumed Birthday Bagel deliverer

If you want a high performance woman, I can go from zero to bitch in less than two seconds.

—**Krystal Ann Kraus**, whose famous quote has inspired everything from book titles to Pinterest boards

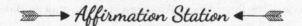

➤➤➤ *Affirmation Station* ◀◀◀

I am living a life of my own design.
I am an action taker.
I am a hard worker.

Behind every successful woman … is a substantial amount of coffee.

—Stephanie Piro, an artist and designer whose relatable comics appear in newspapers around the world

The one important thing I have learned over the years is the difference between taking one's work seriously and taking one's self seriously. The first is imperative and the second is disastrous.

—Dame Margot Fonteyn, who drew international acclaim to England's Royal Ballet through her incredible dancing

I found what I was looking for at Langley. This was what a research mathematician did. I went to work every day for 33 years happy. Never did I get up and say I don't want to go to work.

—Katherine Johnson, a Presidential Medal of Freedom winner and mathematician whose work helped send the first American astronaut into space; she is also known for being one of the three African American graduate students chosen to integrate schools in West Virginia—the 2016 movie *Hidden Figures* is based, in part, on her life

Think bigger! Be a millionaire, don't marry one.

—**Nell Merlino**, the 2000 Forbes Trailblazer who created "Make Mine a Million Business" and "Take Our Daughters to Work Day"

When a neighbor's boy boasted of his exploits at a shooting range, I set out to show that a girl could do as well. So I practiced a lot.

—**Lyudmila Pavlichenko**, a WWII Ukrainian Soviet sniper who achieved over 185 confirmed kills in two and a half months (and over 250 by the end of the war)

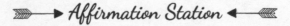 *Affirmation Station*

I enjoy my job and look forward to my career.
I am unstoppable.
I am making my dreams a reality.

My husband was killed in action defending the motherland. I want revenge … for his death and for the death of Soviet people tortured by the fascist barbarians. For this purpose I've deposited all my personal savings—50,000 rubles—to the National Bank in order to build a tank. I kindly ask to name the tank "Fighting Girlfriend" and to send me to the frontline as a driver of said tank.

—**Mariya Oktyabrskaya**, the first woman to be awarded Hero of the Soviet Union, whose tank was damaged in battle after it had taken out numerous opponents (including an enemy anti-tank gun!); she got out and repaired her damaged tank amid gunfire so that she could go after more Nazi soldiers

If you want something in life, you have to go out and get it, because it's just not going to come over and kiss you on your lips.

—**Renee Scroggins**, a member of the band *ESG*, which she started with her sisters and a couple of friends, under the supervision of her mother, before any of them graduated high school

People don't understand the kind of fight it takes to record what you want to record the way you want to record it.

—**Billie Holiday**, also known as Lady Day—and as one of the best jazz singers of all time

If it's a good idea … go ahead and do it. It is much easier to apologize than it is to get permission.

—**Grace Murray Hopper**, a programmer who joined the US Navy during WWII and who later headed the team that made the first computer language compiler; without her work, modern computer programming would not be possible

I was the conductor of the Underground Railroad for eight years, and I can say what most conductors can't say; I never ran my train off the track and I never lost a passenger.

—**Harriet Tubman**, who led hundreds of enslaved Americans to freedom before working as, among other jobs, a Union spy during the Civil War

▼▼▼▼▼▼▼▼▼▼▼▼▼▼▼▼▼▼▼▼▼▼▼▼▼▼▼▼▼▼▼▼▼▼

Badass to the Bone:

Harriet Tubman

In her day, Harriet was lovingly referred to as Moses, for leading her people home to freedom. An escaped slave herself, she pulled off feat after amazing feat and gave freedom to many who would otherwise have never known it. Harriet Tubman was a conductor on the Underground Railroad, perhaps the best that ever was. She is best known for this activity, but she was also a feminist, a nurse, and, for a time, a spy. Her keenest interest was social reform, both for her gender and her people.

Born around 1821 on a plantation in Maryland, Harriet struggled with grand mal seizures after a blow to the head as a child, but the damage from a severely fractured skull didn't stop her from the most dangerous work she could have possibly undertaken: taking groups of slaves to freedom in the north. During her slow recovery from being hit in the head with a two-pound weight by an overseer, she began praying and contemplating the enslavement of blacks, resolving to do what she could, with faith in a higher power. She married John Tubman, a free man, in 1844, and lived in fear that she would be sold into the Deep South. When she heard rumors that she was about to be sold, she plotted her escape, begging John to come with her. He not only refused, but threatened to turn her in.

Harriet escaped to freedom by herself, but immediately plotted to return for her family members, using the Underground Railroad. She ultimately rescued all her family members except John; he had taken a new wife and remained behind. She led more than two hundred slaves to safety and freedom, encouraging her "passengers" with gospel songs sung in a deep, strong voice. She also developed a code to signal danger using biblical quotations and certain songs. Harriet Tubman always outfoxed the whites who questioned her about the groups of blacks traveling with her. She lived in constant threat of hanging, with a forty thousand dollar price on her head, and many close calls. One of the most dramatic incidents shows Harriet's resourcefulness and resolve, when she bought tickets heading south to evade whites demanding to know what a group of blacks were doing traveling together.

Harriet also started connecting with abolitionists in the north, developing a strong admiration for John Brown (she conspired with him in his raid at Harper's Ferry) and Susan B. Anthony. During the Civil War, she nursed black soldiers, worked as a spy for the Union, and even led a raid that freed 750 slaves. After the war, she lived in Auburn, New York, in a house that had been a way station for the Underground Railroad, teaching blacks how to cope with newfound freedom, gathering food, clothing, and money for poor blacks, and founding a home for elderly and indigent blacks. Harriet's last years were spent in abject poverty despite all she had given to others, but she died at the age of ninety-three, having accomplished the task she set herself as a girl. She was the great emancipator, offering her people hope, freedom, and new beginnings.

▲▲▲▲▲▲▲▲▲▲▲▲▲▲▲▲▲▲▲▲▲▲▲▲▲▲▲▲▲▲▲▲▲▲▲▲▲▲▲

⇶→ *Affirmation Station* ←⇷

I will use my success to help others.
I will build my coworkers up as I grow.
I will leave no one behind.

External success has to do with people who may see me as a model, or an example, or a representative. As much as I may dislike or want to reject that responsibility, this is something that comes with public success. It's important to give others a sense of hope that it is possible and you can come from really different places in the world and find your own place in the world that's unique for yourself.

—**Amy Tan**, whose book *The Joy Luck Club* was one of the longest-running *New York Times* bestsellers and has been translated into twenty-five languages

When you've worked hard, and done well, and walked through that doorway of opportunity, you do not slam it shut behind you. You reach back and you give other folks the same chances that helped you succeed.

—**Michelle Obama**, who has worked as a lawyer, assistant commissioner of planning and development for the City of Chicago, and First Lady of the United States

▼▼▼▼▼▼▼▼▼▼▼▼▼▼▼▼▼▼▼▼▼▼▼▼▼▼▼▼▼▼▼

Badass to the Bone:

Michelle Obama

Michelle Obama not only served as the 44th First Lady of the United States of America, but is also an American lawyer, writer, and the founder of *Let's Move!*, an initiative for the prevention of child obesity, as well as an advocate of civil rights for women and LGBT people.

Michelle Robinson was born in Chicago in 1964. In 1985 she graduated from Princeton, and in 1988 she completed a law degree at the prestigious Harvard Law School, after which she worked at Sidley Austin, a Chicago corporate law firm of high repute. Though Sidley didn't usually take on first-year law students as associates, in 1989 they asked Michelle to mentor a summer associate named Barack Obama. When he finished his term as an associate and returned to Harvard, their relationship continued long distance, and in 1992 they married. At the same time, Michelle was evaluating in those years whether a career in corporate law was really what she wanted. She left Sidley Austin and went to work for the City of Chicago, first for the Mayor and then providing her expertise to Valerie Jarrett, the head of the city's planning and development department. In that position she was working for job creation and to bring new life to Chicago's neighborhoods, and after this turning point, she never looked back.

After spending a few years working in hospital administration for the University of Chicago Hospitals, Michelle became First Lady of the United States when her husband won the Presidential election of 2008. In this role, she advocated for military families, working women balancing family with career, and the arts and arts education. Michelle also supported LGBT civil rights, working with her husband for the passage of the Employment Non-Discrimination Act and the repeal of Don't Ask Don't Tell. In 2010, she began to take steps to create a healthier lifestyle for the youth of America with the "Let's Move" campaign to prevent child obesity.

▲▲

I never aimed to be on television or in the press. We all have a personal life, and being a public figure disrupts that.

—**Valentina Tereshkova**, a cosmonaut for the USSR who was first woman in space; she orbited earth forty-eight times in three days

A lot of young girls have looked to their career paths and said they'd like to be chief. There's been a change in the limits people see.

—**Wilma Pearl Mankillers**, an activist for Native American and women's rights who was the first female principal chief of the Cherokee Nation

Vice president—it has such a nice ring to it!

—**Rep. Geraldine Ferraro**, the first female major-party candidate for US Vice President

⋙⟶ *Affirmation Station* ⟵⋘

I inspire others to succeed.
I belong in my position of power.
My actions speak louder than my words.

I don't mind how much my ministers talk—as long as they do what I say.
—**Margaret Thatcher**, who governed for three years as the
first female Prime Minister of Britain

▼▼▼▼▼▼▼▼▼▼▼▼▼▼▼▼▼▼▼▼▼▼▼▼▼▼▼▼▼▼▼▼▼

Badass to the Bone:

Margaret Thatcher

Margaret Thatcher may have drawn fire from critics for
her staunch conservatism, but she has the respect of the world
for her no-nonsense strength and for her rise from greengrocer's
daughter to the first woman Prime Minister of Great Britain.
Thatcher earned all her laurels through sheer hard work, studying
diligently to get into Oxford, where she studied chemistry and
got her first taste of politics. Upon graduation, she got a law

degree, married Dennis Thatcher, and had twins in short order. Her passion for conservative politics increased, and she impressed party members with her zeal and talent for debate. She won a seat in the House of Commons in 1959, and her rise through the party ranks was steady and sure, leading to her election in the eighties as Prime Minister, the first woman ever to head a major Western democracy. Vehemently anti-Communist and anti-waste, she curtailed government with a singular fervor, surprising everyone by going to war with Argentina over the Falkland Islands in 1982. Tough as nails, Margaret explains her modus operandi thusly: "I've got a fantastic stamina and great physical strength, and I have a woman's ability to stick to a job and get on with it when everyone else walks off and leaves."

▲▲▲

It's never too late to be what you might have been.

—**George Eliot**, also known as Mary Ann Evans, who subedited for *The Westminster Review* and was known for her novels' exploration of human psychology

I believe humans get a lot done, not because we're smart, but because we have thumbs so we can make coffee.

—**Flash Rosenberg**, writer, artist, and performer known for her instant art cartoons

I was thirty-two when I started cooking; up until then, I just ate.

—**Julia Child**, who helped American professional and home cooks make difficult French recipes through her TV show and cookbooks

What I know about money I learned the hard way—by having had it.

—**Margaret Halsey**, a witty satirist whose memoir *With Malice Toward Some* humorously critiqued English culture; she later turned her critical eye to American culture, writing most notably about race relations and prejudice

Money, if it does not bring you happiness, will at least help you be miserable in comfort.

—**Helen Gurley Brown**, the editor-in-chief of *Cosmopolitan* for over thirty years; she wasn't afraid to talk about sex, either in *Cosmopolitan* or in her many books

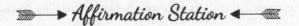

Affirmation Station

I push through negativity and criticism.
I will become rich and successful.
I am capable of managing my money well.

I'm comfortable with money and it's comfortable with me.

—**Diana Ross**, an Academy Award-nominated actress and
singer with several songs hitting number one on pop music
charts, both with her trio *The Supremes* and during her solo career

We don't know who we are until we see what we can do.

—**Martha Grimes**, an American author of British mysteries
who published at least one book a year, every year, for most
of her more than twenty-five-year career

*The state you need to write is that state that others are paying large sums
to get rid of.*

—**Shirley Hazzard**, a transcontinental writer who left her
native Australia with her family at age twenty and later
gained US citizenship; her novel *The Transit of Venus* garnered

international acclaim and was chosen for the 1980 National Book Critics Circle Award

I can never remember being afraid of an audience. If the audience could do better, they'd be up here on stage and I'd be out there watching them.

—**Ethel Merman**, a singer and actress who performed everywhere: from Broadway, to television, to the silver screen

They thought I was a Surrealist, but I wasn't. I never painted dreams. I painted my own reality.

—**Frida Kahlo**, a Mexican artist who, after a bus accident left her severely injured, turned to painting self-portraits and became a political activist

▼▼▼▼▼▼▼▼▼▼▼▼▼▼▼▼▼▼▼▼▼▼▼▼▼▼▼▼▼▼▼▼▼▼

Badass to the Bone:

Frida Kahlo

Frida Kahlo's posthumous pop culture deification has eclipsed the fame of her husband, Mexican muralist Diego Rivera. A total iconoclast, Frida's visceral painting style has an intensity matched by few artists. Her fleshy fruits, torn arteries, tortured birthings, and surreal, imago-packed dreamscapes terrify and mesmerize. Her burning eyes in both self-portraiture and photographs make her hard to forget. Her pain seems to emanate from many wounds—psychic, physical, and romantic.

Born Magdalena Carmen Frida Kahlo y Calderon outside of Mexico City in 1907, Frida contracted polio when she was seven, stunting her right leg. Her father took charge of her recovery from polio, encouraging her to play sports to build back the strength of her right foot and leg. At fifteen, Frida was in a horrendous trolley-car accident, crushing her spine, right foot, and pelvis, leaving her crippled forever. In pain for the remainder of her life, she underwent thirty-five surgeries, the amputation of her gangrenous right foot, and what she deemed as imprisonment bedridden in body casts. Indeed, several of Kahlo's greatest works were done while flat on her back, using a special easel her mother had made for her.

Her tempestuous relationship with world-renowned painter Diego Rivera was also a source of great suffering. Frida and Diego were a very public couple. Coming of age in the wake of the Mexican Revolution, they were both very political; both artists embraced "Mexicanismo," with Frida going so far as to wear traditional Indian peasant costumes at all times, cutting a striking and memorable figure with the rustic formality. Frida's stalwart adherence to all things "of the people" made her a national shero, with papers commenting on her resemblance to an Indian princess or goddess. More than sixty years after her death, Frida and her work hold a fascination that shows no sign of fading. Her dramatic personal style and wild paintings have captured the public's imagination.

▲▲▲▲▲▲▲▲▲▲▲▲▲▲▲▲▲▲▲▲▲▲▲▲▲▲▲▲▲▲▲▲▲▲▲▲

⫸⟶ *Affirmation Station* ⟵⫷

I am powerful and highly capable.

I work for my own gain.

I am good at my job.

Write to amuse? What an appalling suggestion! I write to make people anxious and miserable and to worsen their indigestion.

—**Wendy Cope**, a teacher, writer, television critic, poet, and poetry editor known for her humorous and witty poetry collections, such as *If I Don't Know*

When you perform … you are for minutes heroic. This is power. This is glory on earth. And this is yours nightly.

—**Agnes DeMille**, a ballet dancer and choreographer who brought a stronger narrative to the language of dance

If you have fun at your job, I think you're going to be more effective.

—**Meg Whitman**, a successful businesswoman who served as CEO at both Hewlett-Packard and eBay

The beaten track does not lead to new pastures.

—**Indira Gandhi**, who rose to political popularity through her work to revitalize farming; she later became India's third Prime Minister

▼▼▼▼▼▼▼▼▼▼▼▼▼▼▼▼▼▼▼▼▼▼▼▼▼▼▼▼▼▼▼▼▼▼▼▼▼

Badass to the Bone:

Indira Gandhi

Indira Nehru Gandhi's life mirrors the divided country she governed as the first woman Prime Minister of India. (She was not related to Mahatma Gandhi: her husband, the activist, publisher, and politician Feroze Jehangir Ghandy, changed his last name to "Gandhi" in tribute to his comrade.) As a girl, Indira witnessed up close the birth of modern, independent India under the leadership of Gandhi and her relatives. The Nehrus were a wealthy family who were moved by meeting Gandhi in 1919 and gave up all their possessions to join in the struggle for independence. Indira also organized The Monkey Brigade for preteen revolutionaries and was later beaten cruelly for marching carrying India's flag. She and her family often visited Gandhi, who was "always present in my life; he played an enormous role in my development."

Upon the deaths of their great leader Gandhi and the continued bloodshed during the Partition dividing majority-Hindu India from the new Muslim state of Pakistan, Indira joined India's Congress Party and began to forge her own political sensibility. When India gained independence in 1947, her father became Prime Minister; because he was a widower, he needed Indira to act as his official hostess. While her father was suffering multiple strokes, Indira tacitly acted as Prime Minister. After his death in 1964, she was appointed to India's upper house of Parliament and, after the death of her father's successor in 1966, won the election to become leader of the Congress Party. This made her Prime Minister of the world's largest democracy, and the female leader of a country where women's rights were not a top priority. Immediately she became a role model for millions of India's women, who were traditionally subservient to men.

Indira inherited a land where starvation, civil wars, severe inflation, and religious revolts were a daily reality. She constantly endangered her health by working sixteen-hour days, trying to meet the needs of the second most populated country on earth. Her political fortunes rose and fell; she was booted out of office in 1977, only to be reelected a few years later to her fourth term as Prime Minister. Her controversial birth control program is oftentimes overlooked amid criticisms that she traded political favors in order to hang onto the ministry.

Indira was constantly caught in between the warring factions and divisions of India's various provinces and interests, and the history of her ministry reads like a veritable laundry list of riots, uprisings, and revolutions all playing out on partisan quicksand. Her assassination in 1984 demonstrates this fully. Across India, Sikhs were cursing the name of Gandhi, including some of her personal security guards. Four months later, Indira was shot to death by a Sikh in her garden.

▲▲▲▲▲▲▲▲▲▲▲▲▲▲▲▲▲▲▲▲▲▲▲▲▲▲▲▲▲▲▲▲▲▲▲▲▲

The more you do, the more you are.

—Angie Papadakis, a humorist who served on California boards of education at both the county and state level

So what *does* success mean to you? Take the time to write it down—maybe use one of those sticky notes I know you pulled out when you read the introduction. ☺ Or, you know, you can also just write it here. But write it somewhere where you know you'll look—maybe near your chosen affirmations—and make sure you do look at it. Because whether you feel like you're taking a step forward or three steps back, having your goals in front of you will help you to focus on what you want to achieve—and how you're going to get there.

Chapter Five

Ohana Means Family

"Ohana means 'family.' 'Family' means nobody gets left behind ... or forgotten."

—Lilo, in *Lilo & Stitch*

The world's largest family currently resides in India; counting only dad, moms, and children, it had, as of 2016, over a hundred and thirty members, and that's ignoring more than thirty grandchildren that have been added since last count. According to the Guinness World Records, the largest number of children birthed by a single woman is sixty-nine; the eighteenth-century Russian mother, known only as Mrs. Vassilyeva, was apparently never pregnant with just one kid—she gave birth exclusively to twins, triplets, and quadruplets. I don't know about you, but I don't even want to think about having that many kids. But some mothers love large families, and numbers in the teens are far from unheard of.

⇒⇒ ➤ *Affirmation Station* ◄ ⇐⇐

I am a good parent.
I enjoy spending time with my family.
I am a caring mother.

I could go on about world and national records, but the point is, family can be a big deal. Generally speaking, motherhood is one (and I do mean *one*) of the most important roles that many women will play—and that's not because being a mother is the proper place for every woman, because for some of us, it's really not. Rather, it's important because each and every mother directly influences at least one other person on a daily basis: her child. Parents help create the future in how they raise their kids.

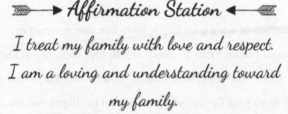

Affirmation Station

I treat my family with love and respect.
I am a loving and understanding toward my family.
I take good care of my children.

Family comes in many shapes and sizes. Not all of us want kids, and not all of us will have them. Some of us can't stand our parents or are estranged from our siblings. But we all have family, biological or otherwise. And every family is important in its own unique way. With that in mind, this is a section where you should really take to heart my advice to pick and choose your affirmations. Because while I know everyone has some sort of family, even if it's made up entirely of furry friends or if it's a family of one, it's important that the affirmations you make regarding your family are true to you.

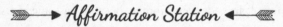

Affirmation Station

I appreciate my parents.
I am encouraging toward my siblings.
I have a loving family in my friends.

Regardless of what your family looks like, the general principles of many families can be maintained: love well, live selflessly, give space where needed, and so on and so forth. What you learn from your family can be expanded to affect how you treat everyone, from your boss, to your friends, to the person who accidentally bumps into you while you're grocery shopping. And what you learn from your own experience with the world can be taken back to your family, too. So do live selflessly. Do give space—for the benefit of others and for the benefit of yourself. And no matter how you love, do it well.

Think of stretch marks as pregnancy service stripes.

—**Joyce Armor**, whose children's poetry focuses on life from
a kid's perspective

Wrinkles are hereditary. People get them from their children.

—**Doris Day**, an actress and singer who helped found animal
welfare organizations like Actors and Others for Animals and
the Doris Day Animal Foundation

*Motherhood is wonderful, but it's also hard work. It's the logistics more than
anything. You discover you have reserves of energy you didn't know you had.*

—**Deborah Mailman**, one of twelve actors offered a two-year
contact with the Sydney Theatre Company and winner of the
AFI Best Actress Award

*Should a woman give birth after thirty-five? Thirty-five is enough kids
for anybody.*

—**Gracie Allen**, an actress whose comedy show with her
husband, *The Burns and Allen Comedy Show*, popularized domestic
situation comedy

Motherhood is tough. If you just want a wonderful little creature to love, you can get a puppy.

—**Barbara Walters**, the first female co-anchor of a network evening news program

▼▼▼▼▼▼▼▼▼▼▼▼▼▼▼▼▼▼▼▼▼▼▼▼▼▼▼▼▼▼▼▼▼

Badass to the Bone:

Barbara Walters

Born September 25, 1929, Barbara is an American broadcast journalist, author, and television personality who has hosted shows including *The Today Show*, *The View*, *20/20*, and the *ABC Evening News*. Barbara attended Sarah Lawrence College in 1951; she obtained a BA in English and then worked at a small advertising agency for a year. After that, she went to work at the NBC network affiliate in New York City doing publicity and writing press releases. Barbara continued on to produce a number of shows, including the *Eloise McElhone Show* until its cancellation in 1954. She then started as a writer on the *CBS Morning Show* in 1955.

Barbara's career began to skyrocket in 1961, when she became a writer and researcher for *The Today Show*; she later moved up to be the show's "Today Girl," a position in which she presented the weather and light news items. At that time, it was still early in the Second Wave of the women's movement; no one took a woman presenting hard news seriously, and there were difficulties with male news anchors like Frank McGee who demanded preferential treatment as she started to cross over into news anchor territory. After McGee passed away in 1974, NBC at last promoted Barbara to the position of co-host—the first woman ever to rise to such a position on any US news program.

Barbara was on a roll. Two years later, she became the first woman to co-anchor any American evening news show on a major network when she joined the *ABC Evening News*, ABC's flagship news program. Walters had a difficult relationship with her co-anchor Harry Reasoner, because he didn't want to have to work with a co-anchor. This led to their team-up lasting only from 1976–1978. Walters became a household name while a co-host and producer at the ABC newsmagazine *20/20* from 1979 to 2004, as well as for her appearances on special reports as a commentator, including Presidential inaugurations and coverage of 9/11. She was also a moderator for the final debate between presidential candidates Jimmy Carter and Gerald Ford. Barbara is famous for her interviews with memorable people, including Fidel Castro, Vladimir Putin, Michael Jackson,

Katharine Hepburn, Anna Wintour, and Monica Lewinsky. In addition to her work at *20/20*, Walters co-created *The View*, a current events talk show hosted solely by women, in 1997. She was a co-host on the show until May 2014, and continues as an executive producer. Barbara Walters was inducted into the Television Hall of Fame in 1989, and in 2007 received a star on the Hollywood Walk of Fame. She has also won Daytime and Primetime Emmy Awards, the Women in Film Lucy Award, the GLAAD Excellence in Media Award, and a Lifetime Achievement Award from the New York Women's Agenda.

▲▲▲

As it stands, motherhood is a sort of wilderness through which each woman hacks her way, part martyr, part pioneer; a turn of events from which some women derive feelings of heroism, while others experience a sense of exile from the world they knew.

—**Rachel Cusk**, an award-winning author who often focuses on family life and parenting

≫➤ *Affirmation Station* ◄≪

I work hard for my children.
I am a good mother.
I am patient with my family.

Never lend your car to anyone to whom you have given birth.

—**Erma Bombeck**, a humorist whose highly popular column "At Wit" focused on suburban housewives

Family is just an accident. … They don't mean to get on your nerves. They don't even mean to be your family, they just are.

—**Marsha Norman**, an award-winning playwright and Pulitzer Prize-winning author whose works include the books of the Broadway versions of *The Color Purple* and *The Secret Garden*

Always be nice to your children because they are the ones who will choose your rest home.

—**Phyllis Diller**, who won the American Comedy Award for Lifetime Achievement after almost forty years as an actress and comedian

Family is a unique gift that needs to be appreciated and treasured, even when they're driving you crazy. As much as they make you mad, interrupt you, annoy you, curse at you, try to control you, these are the people who know you the best and who love you.

—Jenna Morasca, who went on to be a model after being one of the youngest people to win *Survivor*

Family is the most important thing in the world.

—Princess Diana, whose high popularity was outshined only by her humanitarian work and her obvious love for her children

To me luxury is to be at home with my daughter, and the occasional massage doesn't hurt.

—Olivia Newton-John, actress and singer known for her portrayal of Sandy in the film adaptation of *Grease*

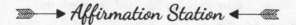

Affirmation Station

I understand the importance of family.
I listen to what my children have to say.
I treasure my family.

My house is very traditional. And I love "shabby chic." It's a very homey-cosy vibe. We spend a lot of time in the kitchen, actually; maybe my kids will be doing their homework or that kind of thing when they get home from school. I love my kitchen.

—**Britney Spears**, one of the youngest women to have six number one albums on the Billboard 200, having started her highly successful singing career in her teens

I think, you know, it was something that I really wanted. I wanted so much to have a son or daughter. We adopted a son. And it was just the most wonderful thing. I think the only thing that was difficult for both Maury and myself were the sleepless nights.

—**Connie Chung**, an award-winning news anchor and one of the first women to co-anchor a major American network newscast

I only do two things in my life, and that's take care of my kids and work. Fortunately, these are my favorite things to do, so it works out.

—**Paula Poundstone**, the first woman to perform standup comedy at the White House Correspondents' Dinner

All those clichés, those things you hear about having a baby and motherhood—all of them are true. And all of them are the most beautiful things you will ever experience.

—**Penelope Cruz**, an Academy Award-winning actress known for her work on *Vicky Cristina Barcelona* and *Vanilla Sky*

All parents want their offspring to be exemplars of virtue and achievement and happiness. But most of all, we want desperately for you to be safe—safe from disease and violence and self-destruction.

—**Estelle Ramey**, a professor and researcher whose published papers include titles such as "Fragility of the Male Sex" and "Male Cycles—They Have Them Too"

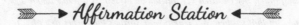

Affirmation Station

Motherhood is a beautiful thing.
I enjoy the small moments with my family.
I appreciate what my parents have done for me.

My favorite thing about motherhood is the outpouring of love that is non-judgmental and beautiful. My daughter just makes me happy, and she motivates me to be a kid again.

—**Christina Milian**, an actress and singer known for *Ghosts of Girlfriends Past* and her hit song "Dip It Low"

To us, family means putting your arms around each other and being there.

—**Barbara Bush**, First Lady from 1988 to 1992; her son Neil's dyslexia inspired her to champion literacy issues, and she founded the Barbara Bush Foundation for Family Literacy in 1989

I love family, my children ... but inside myself is a place where I live all alone and that's where you renew your springs that never dry up.

—**Pearl Buck**, humanitarian and Pulitzer Prize-winning author who was the first female American Nobel laureate, winning the Nobel Prize for Literature

I believe that the greatest gift you can give your family and the world is a healthy you.

—**Joyce Meyer**, an author, TV host, radio host, and president of Joyce Meyer Ministries, a religious multimedia nonprofit

The one thing I missed was never having children. It just wasn't in the cards, I guess.

—**Jeanette MacDonald**, an actress and singer who was a "classical crossover" artist, mixing opera and operetta with show tunes and art songs

Mother of the Children.

—**Honorific title of Fatima al-Fihri**, founder of Al-Qarawiyyin, the world's oldest university (it's been running for 1,200 years!) in Fez, Morocco

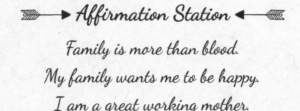

Family is more than blood.
My family wants me to be happy.
I am a great working mother.

My mother was a stay-at-home mom until I was about eleven, when she got a job—and it was like a light came on inside her. It's not wrong to be

passionate about your career. When you love what you do, you bring that stimulation back to your family.

—**Allison Pearson**, an award-winning journalist and author who was recognized as a British Book Awards Newcomer of the Year

Taking responsibility for yourself and your happiness gives great freedom to children. ... Seeing a parent fully embrace life gives the child permission to do the same, just as seeing a parent suffer indicates to the child that suffering is what life is about.

—**Robin Norwood**, a marriage, family, and child therapist who focuses on addiction and the consequences and patterns of unhealthy relationships

I have an office in my house and one about five minutes from my house. I worked solely out of my house for many years, but find, with children, that I have to be in a different ZIP code to think.

—**Cathy Guisewite**, the cartoonist of the highly popular comic strip *Cathy*, which ran for over thirty years

Motherhood has taught me the meaning of living in the moment and being at peace. Children don't think about yesterday, and they don't think about tomorrow. They just exist in the moment.

—**Jessalyn Gilsig**, a small-screen actress of *Friday Night Lights* and *The Practice* fame

I come from a very original family. We didn't have much, but my mother always figured something out. And we were always singing.

—**Freddie Oversteegen**, a member of the Dutch Resistance during World War II; she and her sister would flirt with unsuspecting Nazi collaborators and lead them to another resistance member in the woods, who would then shoot them

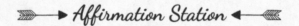

Affirmation Station

*I take the time to live in the moment
with my children.
My family appreciates what I do.
I teach through my actions.*

My children are not royal; they just happen to have the Queen for their aunt.

—**Margaret, Princess of England**, who was commander-in-chief of multiple military units and who worked with over eighty different charities and organizations, ranging from the Royal Ballet to the National Society for the Prevention of Cruelty to Children

If anything, my mother taught me how to sur-thrive. That's my word for it.

—**Carrie Fisher**, a world-renowned actress, novelist, and screenwriter known for her role as Princess Leia in the original *Star Wars* trilogy

Sometimes the strength of motherhood is greater than natural laws.

—**Barbara Kingsolver**, a scientific writer and novelist who established the Bellwether Prize for Fiction

Above the titles of wife and mother, which, although dear, are transitory and accidental, there is the title human being, which precedes and outranks every other.

—**Mary Ashton Livermore**, women's suffrage activist; she was president of the Association for the Advancement of Women and the American Woman Suffrage Association

By and large, mothers and housewives are the only workers who do not have regular time off. They are the great vacationless class.

—**Anne Morrow Lindbergh**, glider pilot and author of over two dozen books

 *Affirmation Station*

I practice selflessness with my family.
My life is better because of my children.
It is okay to take time to be apart from
my family.

The natural state of motherhood is unselfishness. When you become a mother, you are no longer the center of your own universe. You relinquish that position to your children.

—**Jessica Lange**, a model and Academy Award-winning actress known for her roles in *King Kong* and *Blue Sky*

Being a singer is all about me. About ego. Being a mom is all about being selfless—two different worlds.

—**Gwen Stefani**, a multiple Grammy Award-winning singer and fashion designer

Motherhood has most definitely changed me and my life. It's so crazy how drastic even the small details change—in such an amazing way. Even silly things, like the fact that all of my pictures on my cell phone used to be of me at photo shoots—conceited, I know!—but now every single picture on my phone is of Mason.

—**Kourtney Kardashian**, a reality TV star of *The Simple Life* and *Keeping up with the Kardashians* fame

Nothing is better than going home to family and eating good food and relaxing.

—**Irina Shayk**, a model and actress known for her work with *Sports Illustrated* and the Victoria's Secret Fashion Show

I wanted a good relationship with my mother, and I realized I had a choice: Either I could spend all my time angry that she didn't give me the hugs I thought I needed, or I could understand that she hugs differently. It's not a spread-open-the-arms, 'come here' hug. She hugs by sheltering me from her worries.

—**Chandra Wilson**, an award-winning actress and singer known for her roles on *Grey's Anatomy* and in the Broadway revival of *Chicago*

⫸➤ *Affirmation Station* ◀⫷

I am a positive role model.

I am a good provider.

What I have done for my family is enough.

Giving birth was one of my biggest fears, and having Blue forced me to face it. And now I recognize the strength I have. She teaches me to focus on the things that truly matter, like family, and to pay attention to each moment, because they go by so quickly.

—**Beyoncé**, whose pop anthems empower women around the world

▼▼▼▼▼▼▼▼▼▼▼▼▼▼▼▼▼▼▼▼▼▼▼▼▼▼▼▼▼▼▼▼▼▼▼▼▼▼

Badass to the Bone:

Beyoncé

Born in 1981 in Houston, Texas, Beyoncé joined the all-girl R&B group *Girl's Tyme* in 1990; after a few false starts under various names, the group became *Destiny's Child* in 1996. After finding success with several chart-topping *Destiny's Child* singles, she released a solo album in 2003 and has never looked back. She has performed twice at the Super Bowl and sang the national anthem at President Obama's second inauguration. In a 2013 interview with *Vogue*, Beyoncé said that she thought of herself as "a modern-day feminist." That same year, her song "Flawless" featured samples from "We Should All Be Feminists," a *TEDx* talk by Nigerian author Chimamanda Ngozi Adichie.

Since the rise of the Black Lives Matter movement, Beyoncé and her husband have donated millions to it, as well as contributing to the Ban Bossy campaign, which seeks to encourage leadership in girls via social and other media. In April 2016, Beyoncé released a visual album called *Lemonade* as an HBO special. In it, she showed the strength found in communities of African American women as well as in women as a whole. *Lemonade* debuted at number one, making Beyoncé the only artist in history to have all of her first six studio albums reach the top of Billboard's album charts.

▲▲▲▲▲▲▲▲▲▲▲▲▲▲▲▲▲▲▲▲▲▲▲▲▲▲▲▲▲▲▲▲▲▲▲▲▲▲▲

As a housewife, I feel that if the kids are still alive when my husband gets home from work, then hey, I've done my job.

—**Roseanne Barr**, an Emmy Award-winning actress and comedian of *Roseanne* fame

These wretched babies don't come until they are ready.

—**Elizabeth II, Queen of England**, whose reign of over sixty years (and counting!) is the longest in British history

Motherhood is a wonderful thing—what a pity to waste it on children.

—**Judith Pugh**, an award-winning author, art dealer, and poet known for her book *Unstill Life*

No matter what your family looks like, be encouraged by the fact that just as there is no right way to be successful or beautiful, there is no right way to love each other. So if none of these affirmations strike you as something you'd particularly want on a sticky note on your wall, take a moment to sit down and think about your own family. Who are your family members? Where do they live? What do they look like? As you think about your family, think about how you want to treat them, how much you want to interact with them, how much you want to value what they have to say. And as you're thinking about all these things, write your own personal affirmations. There is no wrong answer, and there is no right answer. Just write down the affirmations that are right for you.

Chapter Six

You Are Unstoppable

Did you read that chapter title? You are unstoppable. That's right. You, the person reading this book right now. You really are. And you don't have to feel like it every day for it to be true. Each and every day that you live and breathe, you are proving that you cannot be stopped—that you *refuse* to be stopped.

➤➤ ➤ *Affirmation Station* ◄ ◄◄

I am unstoppable.
I will do what it takes to change the world
for the better.
I learn from every setback.

Every setback teaches you something you will use to leap forward. Every thoughtless criticism adds fuel to your fire. Every single person who tells you that you can't will be proven wrong. And in the end, they don't even matter. That's right—the people who would hold you down, who would prevent you from pursuing your goals and dreams, don't matter. Because they are nothing but hot air. If they lock one door, open another. And if they bar that one, break through a window. Fight your way to the top and take your sisters with you.

⟫⟫⟶ *Affirmation Station* ⟵⟪⟪

*I will use every criticism for my improvement
and benefit.
I will not listen to negativity.
I will not be shaken.*

Because we will not be shaken. Say it with me: *We will not be shaken.* We will not be moved unless we are the ones taking the step. We will not be torn down unless we are tearing negative thinking and false criticisms out of our lives and taping ourselves back up again. And we will not be brought to tears unless those tears are creating a wave for us to ride to victory.

⟫⟫⟶ *Affirmation Station* ⟵⟪⟪

*Every step I take is a step in the right direction.
I will learn from any failures and push forward.
I am changing the world.*

So affirm yourself. Affirm that you are capable because you are. Affirm that you are changing the world because you are. Affirm that you are reaching your goals *because you are*. Write your goals down for the world to see—put them all over your house, make them your screensaver, record them on your phone. Because you will reach them. The only one who stands in your way now is you, so move yourself. You can do it—and you will.

I was set free because my greatest fear had been realized, and I still had a daughter who I adored, and I had an old typewriter and a big idea. And so rock bottom became a solid foundation on which I rebuilt my life.

—J. K. Rowling, a bestselling author and screenwriter whose *Harry Potter* books have inspired children and adults alike

There are stars whose radiance is visible on Earth though they have long been extinct. There are people whose brilliance continues to light the world even though they are no longer among the living. These lights are particularly bright when the night is dark. They light the way for humankind.

—Hannah Szenes, a Jewish poet-turned-soldier who, though taken captive by Nazi forces, refused to give any information up, even in the face of a death sentence by firing squad

So here I stand, one girl among many. I speak not for myself, but so those without a voice can be heard. Those who have fought for their rights. Their right to live in peace. Their right to be treated with dignity. Their right to equality of opportunity. Their right to be educated.

—**Malala Yousafzai**, an advocate for the education of women and girls and winner of the 2014 Nobel Peace Prize; she survived an assassination attempt and, instead of backing down, continued to fight

▼▼▼▼▼▼▼▼▼▼▼▼▼▼▼▼▼▼▼▼▼▼▼▼▼▼▼▼▼▼▼▼▼▼

Badass to the Bone:

Malala Yousafzai

Malala Yousafzai is a Pakistani activist for female education and the rights of girls, as well as the youngest person ever to receive the Nobel Peace Prize. When she heard that BBC News Urdu was looking for a schoolgirl in the Taliban-controlled Swat Valley to anonymously blog about her life and that the girl who had been about to do it had changed her mind due to her family's fear of the Taliban, Malala, who was only in the seventh grade at the time, took on the task. BBC staff insisted she use a pseudonym: she was called "Gul Makai," or "cornflower" in Urdu.

Malala handwrote notes which were then passed to a reporter to be scanned and sent to BBC Urdu by email. On January 3, 2009, her first post went up. As the Pakistani military began pushing into the Swat Valley, she described how the Taliban began shutting down girls' schools. By January 15, the Taliban had issued an edict that no girl was allowed to go to school—and by this point, they had already destroyed over one hundred girls' schools. After the ban went into effect, they continued to destroy more schools. A few weeks later, girls were allowed to attend school, but only at coed schools; girls' schools were still banned, and very few girls went back to school in the atmosphere of impending violence that hung over the area. On February 18, local Taliban leader Maulana Fazlulla announced he would lift the ban on education of females, and girls would be able to attend school until March 17, when exams were scheduled, but they would have to wear burqas.

After Malala finished her series of blog posts for the BBC on March 12, 2009, a *New York Times* reporter asked her and her father if she could appear in a documentary. At this point, military actions and regional unrest forced the evacuation of her hometown of Mingora, and Malala was sent to stay with country relatives. In late July, her family was reunited and allowed to return home, and after the documentary, Malala began to do some major media interviews. By the end of 2009, her identity as the BBC blogger had been revealed by journalists. She started receiving international recognition, and Pakistan awarded her its first National Youth Peace Prize (soon renamed the National Malala Peace Prize in her honor). As things developed, she began to plan the Malala Education Foundation in 2012, the purpose of which would be to help economically disadvantaged girls attend school. But in summer of that year, a group of Taliban leaders agreed to kill her—unanimously. As she rode the bus home in October, a masked gunman shot her; the bullet passed through her head, neck, and shoulder, and wounded two other girls.

Malala barely survived, but was airlifted to a Peshawar hospital, where doctors removed the bullet from her head in five hours. She then received specialized treatment in Europe, paid for by the Pakistani government. Since her recovery, she has continued to speak out both for education for girls and for the rights of women in general. At age seventeen, she was the co-recipient of the 2014 Nobel Peace Prize for her work on behalf of children and young people, sharing the prize with Kailash Satyarthi, a children's rights activist from India. Malala is the youngest Nobel laureate ever. That year she also received an honorary doctorate from University of King's College in Halifax, Nova Scotia. On her eighteenth birthday, she opened a school in Lebanon not far from the Syrian border for Syrian refugees, specifically teenage girls, funded by the nonprofit Malala Fund.

▲▲

I'm not funny. What I am is brave.
—**Lucille Ball**, whose groundbreaking show *I Love Lucy* was one of the first family-based sitcoms; it covered a wide range of issues, including pregnancy, marital issues, women in the workplace, and suburban living, all of which were somewhat controversial at the time

It's a good thing to have all the props pulled out from under us occasionally. It gives us some sense of what is rock under our feet, and what is sand.
—**Madeleine L'Engle**, an author and poet whose award-winning children's books encouraged individuality and bravery

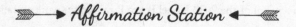

≫⟶ Affirmation Station ⟵≪

I can survive even my greatest fears.
I have important things to say.
I face my fears bravely.

Internalization of a derogatory self-concept always results in a good deal of bitterness and resentment. This anger is usually either turned in on the self—making one an unpleasant person, or on other women—reinforcing the social clichés about them. Only with political consciousness is it directed at the source—the social system.

—Jo Freeman, a lawyer and activist whose involvement in peaceful protests at University of California at Berkeley helped lead to increased freedom of speech at universities nationwide

If people tell you your mother is not Prime Minister anymore, you just turn around and say, "So what? How often has your mother been Prime Minister?"

—Benazir Bhutto, Pakistan's first female Prime Minister, when giving advice to her children as they returned to school

Successful competitors want to win. Head cases want to win at all costs.

—Nancy Lopez, winner of the Women's Sports Foundation's Billie Jean King Contribution Award and four-time LPGA Player of the Year during her golfing career

Don't Pee On My Leg and Tell Me It's Raining

—The title of the first book by Judge Judy Sheindlin, who simultaneously dishes out justice and entertainment on her *Judge Judy* television program

If you always do what interest you, at least one person is pleased.

—Katharine Hepburn, an acting legend and four-time winner of the Academy Award for Best Actress

Just don't give up trying to do what you really want to do. Where there is love and inspiration, I don't think you can go wrong.

—Ella Fitzgerald, the first female African American Grammy Award winner; her incredible jazz singing went on to win her a total of twenty-one Grammys

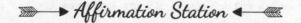

Affirmation Station

I am considerate of myself and others.
I am the only one who needs to understand
my choices.
I will do what I love.

At the end of life, at the end of YOUR life, what essence emerges? What have you filled the world with? In remembering you, what words will others choose?

—Amy Krouse Rosenthal, a writer and YouTuber who gave multiple *TED* talks and who loved doing random acts of kindness; ten days before her 2017 death by ovarian cancer, she published an essay entitled "You May Want to Marry My Husband" in the *New York Times* "Modern Love" column

We can each define ambition and progress for ourselves. The goal is to work toward a world where expectations are not set by the stereotypes that hold us back, but by our personal passion, talents and interests.

—Sheryl Sandberg, Facebook COO and author whose first job out of business school was as chief of staff for the United States Deputy Treasury Secretary

We are born with the seed of joy; it is up to us to nurture it.

—Goldie Hawn, an Academy Award-winning dancer and actress who has graced both the small and silver screens

Optimism for me isn't a passive expectation that things will get better; it's a conviction that we can make things better—that whatever suffering we

see, no matter how bad it is, we can help people if we don't lose hope and we don't look away.

—**Melinda Gates**, cofounder of the Bill & Melinda Gates Foundation, which works to improve education, empower the poor to improve their lives, and combat infectious diseases worldwide

When you walk with purpose, you collide with destiny.

—**Dr. Bertice Berry**, an author, professor, and nationally syndicated talk show host who used humor to discuss racism, sexism, and other difficult topics in order to make a bigger impact on her students

$$\longrightarrow \text{Affirmation Station} \longleftarrow$$

This is my life, and I'm the only one who has to live it.

I walk and act with purpose.

I am capable of making a positive impact.

Magic lies in challenging what seems impossible.

—**Carol Moseley-Braun**, the first female African American elected to the United States Senate

Do what you are afraid to do.

—**Mary Emerson**, an author and philosopher whose love of deep conversation encouraged many of her friends, family members, and readers

Devote today to something so daring even you can't believe you're doing it.

—**Oprah Winfrey**, a philanthropist and media titan whose various productions entertain and inform people worldwide

▼▼▼▼▼▼▼▼▼▼▼▼▼▼▼▼▼▼▼▼▼▼▼▼▼▼▼▼▼▼▼▼▼▼▼▼▼▼

Badass to the Bone:

Oprah Winfrey

Oprah was born to a teenaged mother on a farm in Mississippi in 1954, and her unmarried parents soon separated and left her there in her grandmother's care. She was exceptionally bright; her grandmother taught her to read at the tender age of two and a half, and she was skipped through kindergarten and second grade. At age six, Oprah was sent to live with her mother and three half-siblings in a very rough Milwaukee ghetto. She has said that she was molested as a child, from age nine into her early teens, by men her family trusted.

At twelve, she was again uprooted and sent to live with her father, a barber, in Nashville. This was however a relatively positive time for the young Oprah, who started being called on to make speeches at churches and social gatherings. After being paid five hundred dollars for a speech on one occasion, she knew she wanted to be "paid to talk." She was further bounced back and forth between both her parents' homes, compounding the trauma of the abuse she had suffered. Her mother worked long and irregular hours and was not around much of the time. At fourteen, Oprah became pregnant with a son; he did not survive early infancy. After some years of acting out, including once running away, she was sent to her father to stay for good; she credits her father with saving her with his strictness and devotion, his rules, guidance, structure, and books. It was mandatory that she write a book report every week, and she went without dinner unless she learned five new vocabulary words every day.

Things completely turned around for Oprah. She did well in school and then managed to land a job in radio while still in high school. After winning an oratory contest, she was able to study communications on a scholarship at Tennessee State University, a historically black college. She was a co-anchor of the local evening news at age nineteen and, before long, her emotional verve when ad-libbing took her into the world of TV and radio. She moved to Baltimore, Maryland, in 1976 and struggled as a co-anchor and reporter for the local ABC affiliate; the next year, she found her true medium in talk radio as co-host of *Baltimore Is Talking* and rocketed the show to success. In Baltimore, more people were listening to her than to Phil Donahue, the famed national talk show host. In 1984, she moved on to Chicago and lifted a sleepy local talk show from third place up to first. In 1985, a year after she had taken on *A.M. Chicago*, producer Quincy Jones spotted Oprah on air and decided to cast her in a film he was planning based on Alice Walker's novel *The Color Purple*. Her acting in this extremely well-received film had a meteoric effect on the popularity of her talk show, which was by now *The Oprah Winfrey Show*, and the show gained wide syndication. She had taken a local show and changed its focus from traditional women's concerns and tabloid fodder to issues including cancer, charity work, substance abuse, self-improvement, geopolitics, literature, and spirituality. Oprah launched her own production company in 1986, and was on her way to ruling a media empire.

Oprah launched *O: The Oprah Magazine* in 2000; it continues to be popular. She has spearheaded other publications as well, from four years of *O At Home magazine* to co-authoring five books. In 2008, Oprah created a new channel called OWN: Oprah Winfrey Network and put her self-branded talk show to bed. She has earned the sobriquet of "Queen of All Media" and is accounted as the richest African American and the most pre-eminent black philanthropist in American history. She is at present North America's first and only black multi-billionaire and is considered to be one the most influential women in the world, despite the many setbacks and hardships she endured in early life. She has been awarded honorary doctorates from Harvard and Duke University, and in 2013, Oprah received the Presidential Medal of Freedom from President Barack Obama.

▲▲▲▲▲▲▲▲▲▲▲▲▲▲▲▲▲▲▲▲▲▲▲▲▲▲▲▲▲▲▲▲▲▲▲▲▲▲▲

Never limit yourself because of others' limited imagination; never limit others because of your own limited imagination.

—**Mae Jemison**, first female African American in space; her role as a science specialist led her to conduct motion-sickness and weightlessness experiments on herself and her fellow astronauts

▼▼▼▼▼▼▼▼▼▼▼▼▼▼▼▼▼▼▼▼▼▼▼▼▼▼▼▼▼▼▼▼▼▼▼

Badass to the Bone:

Mae Jemison

In 1981, Mae Jemison earned an MD from Cornell Medical College. During her years at Cornell, she spent some of her time providing primary medical care in Cuba, Kenya, and a Cambodian refugee camp in Thailand; she also kept up her studies of dance at the Alvin Ailey School. She interned at Los Angeles County+USC Medical Center and then worked as a general practitioner. She joined the Peace Corps in 1983 and spent the next two years as the medical officer responsible for corps volunteers' health in Sierra Leone and Liberia, as well as assisting with CDC vaccine research.

After completing her stint with the Peace Corps in 1985, Jemison felt that since fellow Stanford alumna Sally Ride had succeeded in her quest to go to space, the time was ripe to follow her longtime dream, and she applied to join NASA's astronaut training program. The Challenger disaster of early 1986 delayed the selection process, but when she reapplied a year later, Jemison made the cut, becoming the first African American woman ever to do so. She was one of only fifteen chosen out of two thousand applicants. When she joined the seven-astronaut crew of the Space Shuttle Endeavour for an eight-day mission in the fall of 1992, she became the first African American woman in space, logging a total of over 190 hours in space. She conducted medical and other experiments while aloft.

After leaving the astronaut corps in spring of 1993, she was named to a teaching fellowship at Dartmouth, and taught there from 1995 to 2002; she is a Professor-at-Large at Cornell, and continues to advocate for science education and for getting minority students interested in science. She has also founded two companies, the Jemison Group and BioSentient Corp to research, develop, and market various advanced technologies, as well as the Dorothy Jemison Foundation for Excellence, named for her mother, who was a teacher. "The Earth We Share" science camps are among the foundation's initiatives, as well as the "100 Year Starship" project. Jemison has received many awards as well as honorary doctorates from institutions including Princeton, RPI, and DePaul University. Various public schools and a Chicago science and space museum have also been named for her. She has appeared in several TV shows, including an episode of *Star Trek: The Next Generation*, at the invitation of LeVar Burton.

▲▲▲▲▲▲▲▲▲▲▲▲▲▲▲▲▲▲▲▲▲▲▲▲▲▲▲▲▲▲▲▲▲▲▲▲▲

I decided long ago never to walk in anyone's shadow; if I fail, or if I succeed at least I did as I believe.

—**Whitney Houston**, a Grammy Award-winning singer and actress known for her song "I Wanna Dance With Somebody (Who Loves Me)"

Women are not inherently passive or peaceful. We're not inherently anything but human.

—**Robin Morgan**, an author, journalist, and award-winning poet who helped found and lead the contemporary Women's Movement

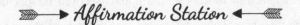 *Affirmation Station*

I can do what has never been done before.
I am unlimited.
I fight for my beliefs.

The only tired I was, was tired of giving in.

—**Rosa Parks**, cofounder of the Rosa and Raymond Parks Institute for Self Development; her famous refusal to give up her bus seat to a white man inspired civil rights protests nationwide, including the Montgomery Bus Boycott, which lasted for over a year

▼▼▼▼▼▼▼▼▼▼▼▼▼▼▼▼▼▼▼▼▼▼▼▼▼▼▼▼▼▼▼▼▼▼▼▼

Badass to the Bone:

Rosa Parks

Rosa Parks gave a human face to the civil rights movement. Born in 1913, Rosa grew up in Pine Level, Alabama, with her schoolteacher mother, Leona. She helped her mother take care of her sickly grandparents and run the household, because Rosa's father had gone to work up north and effectively disappeared from their lives. Later, she moved in with her aunt Fanny and enrolled in the Montgomery Industrial School for Girls, a private school where she was exposed to the liberal ideals of teachers raised in the north. Rosa took her teachers' lessons to heart, as well as the stories her elderly grandparents told about the evils of slavery, sparking a sense of justice that would only grow.

Her involvement in civil rights grew along with her awareness. She was the first woman to start attending the Montgomery chapter of the NAACP and also worked in the effort to register blacks to vote. Rosa often walked home from work to avoid the "back of the bus" issue, until December 1, 1955, when she was returning home from a long day of sewing at a Montgomery department store. The buses from downtown were always fairly crowded and had a section designated for blacks behind the ten rows of seats in the front for white folks. Rosa was sitting in the first row of the "blacks only" section when the white section filled up, leaving a white man without a seat. The tacit understanding was that, in such a scenario, the black person was supposed to stand and let the white person have the seat. The white bus driver called for the four black people in the front row of the black section to get up and let the white man have the row. Rosa refused and the driver called the police.

Her solitary action started a firestorm of controversy, including a bus boycott and protest march led by Martin Luther King Jr. and Coretta Scott King. Though there had been several prior incidents on Montgomery buses, Rosa stuck to her guns and became the pivotal legal case for the burgeoning civil rights movement's attack on segregated seating. Upon going to trial and being found guilty, she refused to pay her fine and appealed the decision. Her actions cost Rosa and her husband dearly; they both lost their jobs and were the recipients of threats to their lives. Undaunted, Rosa worked with the carpooling efforts that enabled blacks to continue their 381-day boycott of the bus system.

The sacrifices of the black community were not in vain, because the US Supreme Court ruled segregated seating to be unconstitutional in 1956. Rosa Parks' courage in that split-second moment when she made her decision is at the very crux of the victorious struggle for African Americans. Rosa worked diligently for the good of her community, traveling and speaking on behalf of the NAACP. She loved to talk to young people about the movement, for the work has truly only begun.

▲▲▲

A great civilization is not conquered from without until it has destroyed itself from within.

—**Ariel Durant**, a Pulitzer Prize-winning co-author, with his wife, of an eleven-volume history entitled *The Story of Civilization*

Only dead fish swim with the stream all the time.

—**Linda Ellerbee**, whose children's news show, *Nick News*, has been honored with numerous awards usually given only to adult news programs

Life should not be a journey to the grave with the intention of arriving safely in an attractive and well-preserved body, but rather to skid in sideways, chocolate in one hand, champagne in the other, body thoroughly used up, totally worn out and screaming, "Woo hoo!! What a ride!"

—**Kate Langdon**, bestselling author and book reviewer

Life is not significant details, illuminated by a flash, fixed forever. Photographs are.

—**Susan Sontag**, a filmmaker, cultural analyst, essayist, and novelist who won the National Book Award for her novel *In America*

➤➤➤ ➤ *Affirmation Station* ◄ ◄◄◄

I create my own path.
I live my life to the fullest.
I am an extraordinary person.

Anything that activates the joy center in the brain makes you happy, and therefore protects you. Oddly enough, that's what they do in Harry Potter: *The nurse gives the kids chocolates when they've been near the Dementors!*

—**Jane Siberry**, a musician and producer known for her hit song "Calling All Angels"

Normal is not something to aspire to, it's something to get away from.

—**Jodie Foster**, an Academy Award-winning actress, producer, and director known for her roles in *Taxi Driver* and *The Silence of the Lambs*

I'm not afraid that the book will be controversial, I'm afraid it will not be controversial.

—**Flannery O'Connor**, a short-story writer and novelist who often wrote about religion in the south

You may be disappointed if you fail, but you are doomed if you don't try.

—**Beverly Sills**, a world-renowned opera soprano who sang with both the New York City Opera and the Metropolitan Opera over the course of her thirty-year career

The fullness of life is in the hazards of life.

—**Edith Hamilton**, whose studies of Greek and Roman literature led her to be one of the first women to attend classes at the University of Munich, Germany

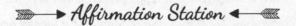

Affirmation Station

I am not afraid of what others think.
I learn and improve from every failure.
I am capable of trying again.

I learned to make my mind large, as the universe is large, so that there is room for paradoxes.

—**Maxine Hong Kingston**, a professor and National Book Award-winning author whose works often focus on the American Asian immigrant community

▼▼▼▼▼▼▼▼▼▼▼▼▼▼▼▼▼▼▼▼▼▼▼▼▼▼▼▼▼▼▼▼▼▼▼▼

Badass to the Bone:

Maxine Hong Kingston

Maxine Hong Kingston's appropriately titled magic realism autobiography, *The Woman Warrior: Memoirs of a Girlhood Among Ghosts*, came out in 1976. Her tale of a Chinese American girl coming of age in California won the National Book Critic's Circle Award and set off a wave of writing by women of color; suddenly Maxine was a literary shero at thirty-six years old. Her subsequent book *China Men* won the same award in 1980, while her 1989 debut novel *Tripmaster Monkey: His Fake Book* thrilled both readers and critics.

Throughout her childhood, Maxine Hong Kingston struggled with being left out of the books she read. There were no stories of Chinese Americans in the Stockton library, and very few that featured girls.

Juxtaposed with the mundane school and laundry work of Maxine's childhood in *The Woman Warrior* are the fantastic imaginings of a girl unfettered by chores and mere reality. Kingston cycles through her mother's women ancestors and speaks frankly of Chinese folk anti-female expressions such as

"When fishing for treasures in the flood, be careful not to pull in girls" and "There's no profit in raising girls. Better to raise geese than girls."

Perhaps, then, it is little wonder that Kingston has come under the strongest attacks from those within her own culture. Several Chinese men have gone after Maxine, criticizing her for everything from her creative license with Chinese legends to her marriage to a white man. Clearly, Kingston stuck a nerve with the power of her writing, touching on the critical issues of race and gender in a way that has caused it to become "the book by a living author most widely taught in American universities and colleges," notes former Poet Laureate Robert Hass. In *Warrior Woman*, Kingston's protagonist's inner battle rages silently within the confines of her mind—race, gender, spirit, identity, straddling the duality of a culture that devalues girls at the same time the legends say "that we failed if we grew up to be but wives or slaves. We could be heroines, swordswomen."

▲▲▲▲▲▲▲▲▲▲▲▲▲▲▲▲▲▲▲▲▲▲▲▲▲▲▲▲▲▲▲▲▲▲▲▲▲

We have too many high-sounding words, and too few actions that correspond with them.

—**Abigail Adams**, a First Lady of the United States whose counsel greatly aided her husband in his pursuit of the Presidency; she was so influential over her husband's policy that she was sometimes known as "Mrs. President"

You don't make progress by standing on the sidelines, whimpering and complaining. You make progress by implementing ideas.

—**Rep. Shirley Chisholm**, the African American to serve in Congress and to run in a major-party Presidential primary; her whose platform included focuses on education and social justice

▼▼▼▼▼▼▼▼▼▼▼▼▼▼▼▼▼▼▼▼▼▼▼▼▼▼▼▼▼▼▼▼▼

Badass to the Bone:

Shirley Chisholm

Born in the borough of Brooklyn, New York, in 1924, Shirley spent seven years in Barbados with her grandmother, Emily Seale. She credits the "stiff upper lip" and excellent education she received in Barbados as giving her an advantage when she returned to the United States. Shirley garnered many scholarship offers upon her graduation from high school, choosing Brooklyn College to study psychology and Spanish with the intention of becoming a teacher. She got involved with the Harriet Tubman Society, where she developed a keen sense of black pride. Acing every course, she received a lot of encouragement to "do something" with her life. A Caucasian political science professor urged her to pursue politics, a daunting idea at the time. But the seed was planted.

In the sixties, Shirley stepped into the political arena, campaigning for a seat in the State Assembly in her district. She won the Democratic seat in 1964 and began the first step in a history-making career, winning again in '65 and '66. Then she decided to run for Congress. Even though she was up against a much more experienced candidate with deep-pocketed financial backing, Shirley prevailed; she was aware that there were thirteen thousand more women than men in the district and quickly mobilized the female vote. She also underwent surgery for a tumor at this time, but went back to work immediately, quickly earning a reputation as one of the hardest-charging black members of the House.

Even in Congress, the race issue reared its head. She was assigned to the Agricultural Committee to work with food stamp distribution because she was a black woman. Shirley didn't take this lying down and fought to get off that committee, moving on to Veteran's Affairs and finally to the Education and Labor Committee, where she believed she could really do some good. Known for her straight-shooting verbal style and maverick political ways, she always saw herself as an advocate for her constituency, seeking to be the voice of those traditionally overlooked by politics: Hispanics, Native Americans, drug addicts, and gay activists.

As a presidential candidate for the 1972 Democratic nomination, she placed women's rights at the center of her campaign, announcing herself as a serious contender and not a "gimmick" candidate. Although she failed to get the nod, her primary run did make her a national spokesperson for the civil and women's rights movements. Afterwards, she helped create the National Political Congress of Black Women and taught, lectured, and authored two books, *Unbought and Unbossed* and *The Good Fight*. Shirley Chisholm was at the forefront of obtaining real political power for African American woman.

▲▲

Some people with awful cards can be successful because of how they deal with the tragedies they're handed, and that seems courageous to me.

—Judith Guest, who quit teaching to finish her first novel, which she counts as the most important decision she's made in her writing career

Revolution begins with the self, in the self.

—Toni Cade Bambara, an award-winning author and director of the *Theater of the Black Experience*

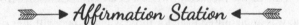

Affirmation Station

I turn my complaints into solutions.
My situation does not define me.
My actions will lead to positive change.

Never do things others can do and will do, if there are things others cannot do or will not do.

—Amelia Earhart, the first pilot to fly a plane across both the Atlantic and Pacific oceans and first woman to fly across the Atlantic Ocean

Remember, each one of us has the power to change the world. Just start thinking peace, and the message will spread quicker than you think.

—**Yoko Ono**, a world-renowned artist and musician who started the LennonOno Grant for Peace Award

▼▼▼▼▼▼▼▼▼▼▼▼▼▼▼▼▼▼▼▼▼▼▼▼▼▼▼▼▼▼▼▼▼

Badass to the Bone:

Yoko Ono

One of the most controversial figures in rock history, Yoko Ono was an acquired taste for those willing to go with her past the edge of musical experimentalism. Unfairly maligned as the woman who broke up the *Beatles*, she is a classically trained musician and was one of New York's most cutting edge artists before the Fab Four even cut a record. Born in Tokyo in 1933, she moved to New York in 1953 and attended Sarah Lawrence, but even then had trouble finding a form to fit into; her poetry was criticized for being too long, her short stories too short.

Soon, Yoko was making a splash with her originality in post-Beatnik Greenwich Village, going places even Andy Warhol hadn't dared with her films of 365 nude derrieres, her performance art (inviting people to cut her clothes off her), and her bizarre collages and constructions. Called the "High Priestess of the Happening," she enthralled visitors to her loft with such art installations as tossing dried peas at the audience while whirling her long hair. Yoko Ono had an ability to shock, endless imagination, and a way of attracting publicity that P. T. Barnum himself would've envied!

When John Lennon climbed the ladder on that fateful day to peer at the artistic affirmation Yoko created in her piece "Yes," rock history was made. Their collaborations—*The Plastic Ono Band*, Bed-Ins, Love-Ins, and Peace-Ins, not to mention their son Sean Lennon—have created a legacy that continues to fascinate a world that has finally grudgingly accepted and respected this bona fide original. Yoko's singing style—howling and shrieking in a dissonant barrage—has been a major influence on the *B52s* and a generation of riot grrl bands. … Much of Yoko's musical output in the seventies was on the theme of feminism; her song "Sisters O Sisters" is one of her finest works, a reggae-rhythm number. Yoko's sheroism lies in her intense idealism and her commitment to making this a better world.

▲▲▲▲▲▲▲▲▲▲▲▲▲▲▲▲▲▲▲▲▲▲▲▲▲▲▲▲▲▲▲▲▲▲▲▲

Aerodynamically, the bumble bee shouldn't be able to fly, but the bumble bee doesn't know it so it goes on flying anyway.

—**Mary Kay Ash**, founder of the highly successful cosmetics company, Mary Kay, Inc.

The strange thing about life is that though the nature of it must have been apparent to every one for hundreds of years, no one has left any adequate account of it. The streets of London have their map; but our passions are uncharted. What are you going to meet if you turn this corner?

—**Virginia Woolf**, author and feminist known for her works *Mrs. Dalloway* and *A Room of One's Own*

Life is better than death, I believe, if only because it is less boring, and because it has fresh peaches in it.

—**Alice Walker**, a Pulitzer Prize-winning author, poet, essayist, and activist known for her novel *The Color Purple*

Take the affirmations you have written down, the ones from this book, and any you created for yourself, and wear them like armor. Anyone who wants to get to you has to get through your unwavering self-confidence, your powerful love, your strength and beauty, your inner drive, your family support, and your raw power. And the more you affirm yourself, the stronger that armor will be. So don't give up. Don't give in. Live your life the way *you* want to live it.

Journaling

What are your goals? How will you affirm them?

_____

_____

_____

_____

_____

_____

_____

_____

_____

_____

_____

_____

_____

_____

What baby steps will you take this week to kick-start your positive life changes?

_____

_____

_____

_____

_____

_____

_____

_____

_____

_____

_____

_____

_____

_____

_____

_____

_____

What is an area in your life that could use a confidence boost? What affirmations can help give you that boost?

_____

_____

_____

_____

_____

_____

_____

_____

_____

_____

_____

_____

_____

_____

_____

_____

_____

What changes do you want to see in your love life?
What affirmations can help you make those changes?

_____

_____

_____

_____

_____

_____

_____

_____

_____

_____

_____

_____

_____

_____

Draw a line down the center of this page, leaving some space at the bottom. On the left side of the line, describe your current self-image. On the right, describe the self-image you wish you had. In the space at the bottom, write affirmations to help you shift to your future self-image.

_____

_____

_____

_____

_____

_____

_____

_____

_____

_____

_____

_____

Write down your goals for your career.
What affirmations will help you reach these goals?

_____

_____

_____

_____

_____

_____

_____

_____

_____

_____

_____

_____

_____

_____

_____

_____

Describe your family. Remember that family does not necessarily require blood relation. What affirmations can you use to keep family interactions positive and loving?

_____

_____

_____

_____

_____

_____

_____

_____

_____

_____

_____

_____

_____

_____

What is stopping you from achieving your goals? Draw a line down the center of this page. On the left, list the obstacles you are facing. On the right, list affirmations and actions you will use to overcome these obstacles.

_____

_____

_____

_____

_____

_____

_____

_____

_____

_____

_____

_____

_____

List five things you will get done before you go to sleep tonight, leaving space between each task. When the day has finished, record what you did and how you felt after accomplishing this goal.

_____

_____

_____

_____

_____

_____

_____

_____

_____

_____

_____

_____

_____

_____

*What new habits do you want to create? How will you
implement these habits in small steps each day?*

_____

_____

_____

_____

_____

_____

_____

_____

_____

_____

_____

_____

_____

_____

_____

How can you realistically lead a healthier life?
What small steps will you take each day to implement
these ideas?

_____

_____

_____

_____

_____

_____

_____

_____

_____

_____

_____

_____

_____

_____

_____

_____

*Who are you thankful for, and why? How can you be
kind to these people in the next few days?*

_____

_____

_____

_____

_____

_____

_____

_____

_____

_____

_____

_____

_____

_____

What is stressing you out today? What positive affirmations can you use to combat these stressors?

_____

_____

_____

_____

_____

_____

_____

_____

_____

_____

_____

_____

_____

_____

_____

_____

What is an activity that makes you happy? Why does it make you happy? How can you increase that happiness in your life?

_____

_____

_____

_____

_____

_____

_____

_____

_____

_____

_____

_____

_____

_____

_____

Pick an inspiring quote. Why does it inspire you?
How will you take advantage of that inspiration today?

_____

_____

_____

_____

_____

_____

_____

_____

_____

_____

_____

_____

_____

_____

_____

Write down a quote that you disagree with.
How can you learn from this different perspective?

_____

_____

_____

_____

_____

_____

_____

_____

_____

_____

_____

_____

_____

_____

Turn on an instrumental song. As you're listening, write down what the song makes you think of. What can you learn about yourself from these thoughts?

_____

_____

_____

_____

_____

_____

_____

_____

_____

_____

_____

_____

_____

_____

List five positive actions that you can take in the next five minutes. Complete these actions, then write about how your life was improved by these small steps in the right direction. How can you use this momentum to push yourself forward?

_____

_____

_____

_____

_____

_____

_____

_____

_____

_____

_____

_____

_____

What is something that you feel guilty about but cannot change? What are some affirmations you can use to slowly quiet your guilt so that you can learn from these mistakes without losing confidence?

_____

_____

_____

_____

_____

_____

_____

_____

_____

_____

_____

_____

_____

_____

_____

_____

Write down your favorite encouraging quote.
What are five ways you can encourage someone today?

_____

_____

_____

_____

_____

_____

_____

_____

_____

_____

_____

_____

_____

_____

_____

_____

About the Author

Becca Anderson comes from a long line of preachers and teachers from Ohio and Kentucky. The teacher side of her family led her to become a woman's studies scholar who runs *The Blog of Awesome Women*. An avid collector of meditations, prayers, and blessings, she helps run a "Gratitude and Grace Circle" that meets monthly at homes, churches and bookstores. Becca Anderson credits her spiritual practice with helping her recovery from cancer and wants to share this with anyone who is facing difficulty in their life. The author of *Think Happy to Stay Happy*, *Real Life Mindfulness*, and *Every Day Thankful*, Becca Anderson shares her inspirational writings and suggested acts of kindness at https://thedailyinspoblog.wordpress.com/.

Awesome Books for Your Awesome Life!

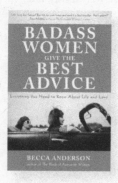

Badass Women Give the Best Advice: Everything You Need to Know About Love and Life

Every Day Thankful: 365 Blessings, Graces and Gratitudes

Plan Be!: Awesome Affirmations for Living an Awesome Life

Real Life Mindfulness: Meditations for a Calm and Quiet Mind

The Book of Awesome Women: Boundary Breakers, Freedom Fighters, Sheroes and Female Firsts

Think Happy to Stay Happy: The Awesome Power of Learned Optimism

CPSIA information can be obtained
at www.ICGtesting.com
Printed in the USA
BVHW052248071122
651351BV00002B/2